Hints On Photoplay Writing

COMPILED FROM THE SERIES OF
ARTICLES WRITTEN BY

CAPTAIN LESLIE T. PEACOCKE

FOR PHOTOPLAY MAGAZINE AND
WHICH WERE PUBLISHED
1915-1916

———

This pocket-size volume contains all that
can be taught of the art of writing
and the business of marketing
moving picture scenarios

———

TABLE OF CONTENTS

CAPT. PEACOCKE

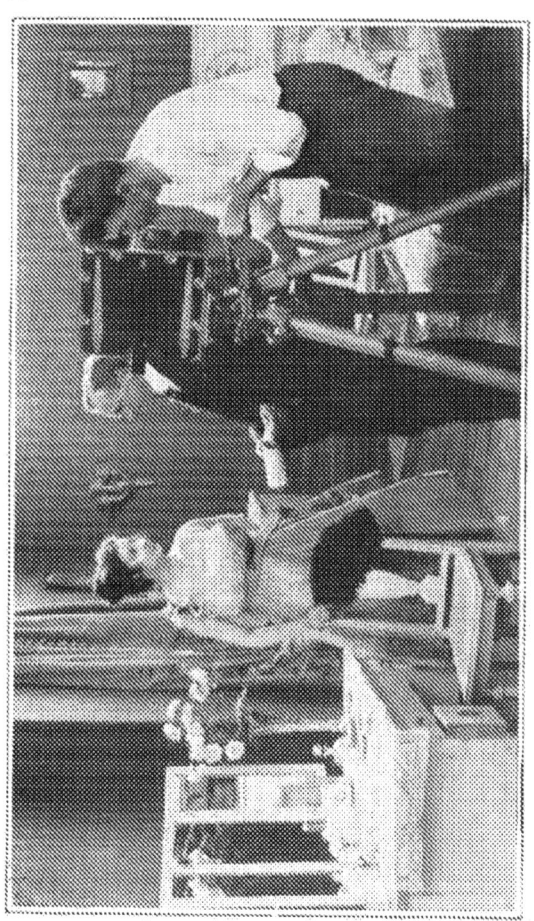

STUDIO SCENE

I

INTRODUCTORY BRIEFS

IF you have a strong, original plot, you already have ninety-nine per cent of a successful scenario.

It isn't often a beginner's first attempt is successful. If you are in earnest you will keep on.

Your head is usually a better place to work over your half-baked plot than pencil and paper or the ear of a friend. O beware of the ear of a friend!

Before the scenario comes the making of the synopsis. A good synopsis won't sell a poor scenario, but many a good scenario has lost a hearing because of a poor synopsis.

The briefer, crisper, more pointed and compact a synopsis is, the friendlier will be its reception by the scenario editor, who is a very, very, *very* busy man. Sometimes his mail brings him as many as four hundred 'scripts in a day. Be brief with him and he may be good to you. A synopsis of fifty words is just fifty times better than a synopsis of twenty-five hundred words—which never in the wide world will be read unless it is submitted in lieu of a scenario.

Beginners will do well to aim at one and two-reel stories, instead of falling down on four and five-reelers and longer. You can't be a steamship captain without experience.

Don't strain yourself to concoct a bizarre plot. The successful one or two-reel story may be living next door to you behind your neighbor's curtains. Leave the big attempts to the big, experienced men, at the start. Moreover, the public loves a simple, homely story if the heart interest be strong. Remember "Shore Acres" and "The Old Homestead." They're running yet.

Never, under any circumstances, take your plot from anything that has been printed. If yours isn't an original plot— that is, a plot originating with you—the scenario readers will recognize the fact at a glance and return it. They are paid to know what has been printed.

Don't fool with fine writing or attempts at fine writing. You are just clogging the wheels that may be grinding grist for you. Tell your story as simply as you know how.

It is good general advice to beginners to submit nothing but two synopses, one very brief, the other extended to cover the story in its important details, instead of attempting the creation of a professional scenario 'script. Many producers so prefer. Of course if you feel competent—go ahead.

Steer clear of vice stories and stories with unhappy endings. A story with tears instead of smiles in its tail has to be a wonder to get by the scenario editor, the managing director, and the producer.

If you don't understand a subject, you've no business to write about it. The world is full of experts in their lines.

You can't sell a scenario unless it's typewritten. You can't even get it read.

Don't send loose stamps for return of manuscript. Enclose self-addressed stamped envelope. It's a rule of the game.

Let "slapstick" comedies alone. The world's pretty weary of them anyhow, and any that are needed will be manufactured "on the inside."

Don't essay costume plays. Wasting your time.

War plays ditto.

Don't send in July a scenario that has to be made in December or January. Be as seasonable as the seasons.

Don't write Bible or allegorical stories and expect to sell them. You can't.

The best teacher of scenario writing is the moving picture screen itself. Watch the different pictures, as many of them as you can see; study them, ponder their theses and thats and whys, and you will learn.

Be careful about making your scenarios so lavish or difficult that their expense to the producer will prevent their acceptance.

If you can't sell your own scenario, no agent can sell it for you. Don't throw away your money and time on middlemen.

Don't become discouraged. Faint heart ne'er won scenario check.

II

THE PLOT'S THE THING

A FINE Production! An interesting "Star"! Acting Splendid! Good Photography! Beautiful Stage Settings and Scenery! Capably Directed! Details almost Perfect! *BUT—"What was it all about?"*

That is the questioning wail you hear from all sides when the average photoplay is under discussion. "What was it all about?"

Everything good, except *THE STORY*.

If the production is a so-called "Feature" in four or more reels, then 9 times out of 10 it will be an adaptation of a mildewed, timeworn stage play, or of a fiction book with a plot as weak as church-social punch.

If the production is a short, one or two-reel subject, then 7 times out of 10 it will have emanated from a "staff-writer" who is urged into turning out at least two "original" photoplays a week, or else stand an excellent chance of losing his job.

Dozens of splendid original stories may be among the hundreds submitted through the mail by capable free-lance writers, but will never be brought to the eye of the scenario editor or of a producing director, because if the outside material submitted should prove to be consistently better than that turned out by the salaried writers, the latter would naturally suffer.

Staff-writers cannot do it all, ·and the sooner the real heads of the film-producing companies begin to realize this, the better for the moving picture industry. They must have staff-writers—even more than

---

DON'T make the mistake of thinking the market success of your submitted scenario rests upon technical instructions about how to build the scenes in front of the camera. Studio department heads are paid to take care of that. What they want from you is an idea.

---

they now employ—but they must be con-
structionists, not hack photoplay writers.
They may be called upon to write stories
on special subjects when such are required,
and should be capable of turning out a
good story in such cases; as the majority
of the staff-writers at present employed
undoubtedly are; but their chief duties
should be in reconstructing good original
stories that reach the scenario departments
from various sources, and adapting such
plays and books as the management has
decided upon producing.

Original stories! Original photoplays
especially written for the screen by competent scenario writers! That is the urgent
need of the film manufacturing companies.
It had to come, as we all knew it would.
Nearly all the stage plays and published
books that lent themselves to film adaptation have been produced or are in the
course of production, and now the eyes of
the big men in the moving picture industry
are turning on the individual who has been
patiently waiting for recognition,—the scenario writer with original ideas, who has

been devoting thought and study to the screen.

Now, the novice who is just starting in to write scenarios will naturally argue that this may be all very fine for the scenario editors, staff-writers, and others who have already won recognition from the film companies, but that those who have yet their spurs to win will receive as scant treatment as ever before.

This is not so. Good, original, virile, human, up-to-date stories, well worked out into scenes, with logical continuity, are what the heads of the firms and the producing directors are ardently fishing for, no matter from what source they come. It is becoming an open market for the competent scenario writer, and is becoming more so every day.

Remember, it is not only in your plots that you must be original. It is also in the little touches which the spark of genius within you may inspire that makes for striking contrast in your proposed production to others you may have seen.

Try and evolve novel situations and effects throughout your scenario. These may be wrought by carefully-thought-out "close-ups" and scenic effects which may occur to you in your daily or nightly walks. Try and look at things with a "camera eye;" a knowledge of photography is very helpful in scenario writing. The camera-man plays a very important part in a production; more so than producers appear to realize. A capable camera-man is quite as important to the success of a film production as is the director; in fact, more so, and although somewhat late in the day, this is being acknowledged by the heads of the firms producing moving pictures.

. You must not get the idea into your head that photoplay writing is easier work than short-story writing. It is not. As a photoplay has to be evolved nowadays, I think that short-story writing is by far the easier of the two. Of course you do not have to battle with "dialogue," or descriptive matter, but you have to create suspense.

The *plot* is the thing. The *original plot*. Have you one? If you have, guard it as carefully as the pupil of your eye. Be careful to whom you submit it. Do not whisper it, even to your best friend. An original plot for a photoplay means big money these days; and, like a rare postage stamp, gains in value every day—provided, of course, that some one else does not hit upon the same idea and market it before you do. There is, unfortunately, always that danger to be reckoned with.

I do not believe there is much danger in having an original plot pirated by the members of any reputable scenario department, because if a staff-writer should be once caught and denounced as a literary pirate, he would be blacklisted from New York to the Pacific Coast. And, nowadays, "readers" are being employed by the foremost film producing companies, and the staff-writers do not have the handling of scripts submitted by free-lance writers until they have passed through the readers' hands, so the purloining of a submitted plot would surely be detected, if any staff-writer felt inclined to be dishonest; which I very much doubt, because (with one exception) I have always found them to be as honorable a set of ladies and gentlemen as one might meet in a year's march.

But if you submit an original plot to some

of the fake concerns which claim to be able to find a market for photoplays—*look out!* You may as well take off your hat to your original plot and say "Good-bye"—or perhaps *"Au revoir"* would be the more sensible parting, because you will probably meet it on the screen, but *not* with your own name attached to it as the author of the play.

Now, as regards the current or future market for photoplays, in which all writers are interested, it is becoming more difficult to give bona fide advice to free-lance writers, because the producing companies are so continually changing the subjects and the lengths of their productions.

THE story is the main thing! Studios are literally pestered with "correctly constructed plots" which have nothing good about them but their technique — commonly picked up at second hand. Technique never put soul into a plot and never will. Remember that and—remember that!

Some of the old reliable companies are abandoning the one and two-reel pictures altogether, and are going in solely for five-reel features, while others, having found the so-called "features" a losing game, are reverting to the short subjects. They are like the Old Woman Who Lived in a Shoe. They don't know what to do, and for advice they are relying largely on a fickle public; so it is on that same fickle jade the writers have to depend, and, believe me, she keeps us all guessing!

A number of writers are submitting and marketing their synopses only, leaving it to scenario departments to work their plots into proper scenario form. Perhaps they are wise in doing this; some scenario editors prefer it.

Merely doping out your story, scene by scene, and only bearing in mind its logical continuity, does not constitute a worthwhile photoplay. We see many such produced on the screen, and they, somehow, fall flat. There is something missing. They are eggs without salt. They are homes without children. They may be good stories; they may please us, and all that—but they lack something badly, and that something is the Master Touch.

Now, you can give your story that Touch if you will only give the thought and care that is necessary when evolving your scenario. Remember that there may be as much expression depicted by a "close-up" of a hand or a foot, deftly inserted in a dramatic scene, as there may be in a semi-distant view of a whole human body. And, above all, *create suspense.*

You do not always require a strong dramatic situation or climax to create suspense; but you should keep it up right throughout your whole scenario, if you can. It's the little deft touches that count. Put salt upon your egg—bring in the little touches of

THE average magazine story contains as much plot as the average long book or stage play, and the average scenario which is evolved by the writers who have made it their business contains more originality than either of those two.

Nature that strike the human chord in every country in the universe.

A "close-up" of an infant's tiny foot, with the weeny toes wiggling, will entice a lump to every woman's throat—if her heart is not a stone. A man may smile at the flashed scene, but if he's a father, and away from home, it won't seem altogether a ridiculous thing to him. It has struck a chord within. It's that touch of Nature which makes the whole world kin!

I cannot too strongly advise magazine story writers to reserve the film rights to any stories which contain plots original and strong enough to be made into film productions. Sell the fiction rights *only* to the magazines. Very often the film rights will net you thrice the amount you may receive for the fiction rights, and surely the author is the one who should be entitled to all that may accrue from the efforts of his or her brain.

I, myself, adapted a magazine story for a five-reel feature not long ago, for which the film-producing company paid one hundred dollars to the publishers of the magazine. I know the author of the story, and he told me that he sold *all rights* to the publishers for thirty-five dollars, and he felt, naturally, aggrieved. However, he will be wiser in the future.

On the other hand, if you can write fiction, which every photoplay writer should endeavor to do, you should reserve all fiction rights to the plot embodied in your scenario. You are entitled to reap all the benefits, and no fair-minded scenario editor will refuse you if you demand the reservation when submitting your script.

III

CONSTRUCTION, TECHNIQUE, TITLES

DO not attempt to be "literary." Stick to simple language;—the simpler, the better,—as the reader is anxious to get at the heart of the story and cares nothing about literary style.

Next we must have our cast of characters. Their names should be short, as we will find in working out the scenes of the photoplay that short names are easier to write and to remember. How much easier it is to write, "May Stubbs," perhaps fifty times during the working out of a script, than to have to worry with "Virginia Maltravers" through the same amount of scenes. This we soon learn from experience.

Then we must state the age of each character, and append a short description of each one, and state what relation one bears to the other, if any.

We must only deal with the main characters at first;—the ones we are certain of using;—and then, later, when the minor auxiliary characters crop up, as they are more than apt to, we can add them to our already formed list. This can be done when our photoplay is finished.

Then we start to work out our scenes, introducing our characters in the strongest, but most logical way possible. We must make each scene stand out by itself, yet tell the action in as few words as possible. Any scenes which threaten to be unduly long should be broken up by "flashing back" to some other scene which is helping to carry the story, and then returning again to the scene and continuing it to its conclusion.

Now we will try and outline as clearly as we can, without being too technical, how the scenes of the photoplay should be evolved.

In these, as in the synopsis, brevity allied with clearness is the chief essential. No attempt should ever be made to too clearly depict a scene. A very great deal must be left to the common sense of the producing director.

To convey what I mean, I will depict the

following few scenes, which I take at random from a produced photoplay, and will then explain why the scenes and the action embodied in them are sketched so very briefly.

Scene 1—Park—Mary (a flirt) seated on bench reading. Charlie approaches. Flirtation. Eyes only. Charlie walks past and off. Mary rises, walks off, opposite direction.

Scene 2—Park—Close-up of Charlie looking back and smiling conceitedly.

Scene 3—Park Gates—Close-up of Mary looking back and smiling encouragingly.

Scene 4—Street—Mary walking. Meets Charlie. He passes her. She drops her handkerchief. He picks it up and presents it to her. Raises his hat and walks on. Mary continues walking. Charlie turns back and follows her.

Scene 5—Exterior of Swell Restaurant—Mary appears and enters. Then Charlie appears. Takes out purse; examines contents. Is satisfied he can meet any emergencies, and enters restaurant.

Scene 6—Interior of Restaurant—Mary at table. Waiter taking her order. Charlie enters. Sits at adjacent table. Starts to study the menu. Cut scene.

Scene 7—Street—Robert (Mary's fiance) appears, walking rapidly; up to camera, and past it. Cut back to

Scene 8—Interior of Restaurant—Mary and Charlie still seated at adjacent tables. He moves to her table and orders bottle of wine. Waiter leaves room. They flirt. Charlie kisses her. Robert enters. Trouble. Ending with Charlie lying senseless and Robert escorting Mary out of restaurant.

Here, now, we have eight scenes, and all ⁓described so clearly, I hope, that anyone with average intelligence can understand them. The topic is not a very well chosen one, perhaps, but it is a very common one and easily grasped by all.

The action runs smoothly throughout and does not need a single "subtitle" to assist it along. Subtitles must be used as little as possible. A scenario full of subtitles is one that is badly written. A writer should be able to make the action in the continued scenes convey the story. However, that is a subject we must deal with later and at more length. We will now diagnose the scenes described above.

Scene 1 is described by the single word "Park." That is enough. There is no use in trying to describe the sort of park you may have in mind. The director will select his own location, but he will have sense enough to know that it must contain a path, and that there is a bench at the edge of the path for Mary to sit on. You may trust to the director to pick out a suitable location and to know the meaning of the single word "Flirtation." The majority of them are married men and have learned how to use their eyes in early youth, the same as other people.

Scenes 2 and 3 are described as "Close-Up," which means to convey that they are the figures of Mary and Charlie taken at very close range of the camera.

MANY embryonic photoplay writers—and some not so embryonic in the game—are hazy in their minds about the meaning of certain technical terms in the make-up of a scenario. It is well, though by no means essential, to have a little information on this subject.

These "close-ups," as they are called, should be frequently used in a scenario, as they bring the audience in close touch with the characters and help to relieve the monotony of distant and half-distant scenes. This you will readily grasp if you are a close observer of the pictures you see on the screen, which every scenario writer must be, if she or he hopes to succeed.

Scene 4 is a Street. That is sufficient. Here again the director will select his own location. Never attempt to describe ordinary scenes. You can never tell where the producing company will be located. It may be in the heart of New York city, or the woods of New Jersey, or the sun-kist slums of Los Angeles, or the boulevards of Chicago. No matter where he may be, you may rest assured the director will select the best site that offers.

Scene 5 needs no comment. It is taken for granted that Mary would not enter a cheap restaurant. She was reading in the park and is therefore a girl of leisure and probably wealthy. No doubt, well dressed, or Charlie would not have wanted to flirt with her or to examine the state of his

finances to see whether he could afford to
treat her to a lunch in the restaurant.

Scene 6 is also very clear. At the close
of the scene you will notice the words:
"Cut Scene." This means to convey that
as soon as Charlie starts to study the menu
the scene is finished—i. e., the camera stops
working.

Scene 7 is another Street scene. At the
end of the scene you will notice the words:
"Cut back to." This explains that your
next scene will be the same as number 6.
You cut back to the preceding scene.

Scene 8 is therefore the same as scene 6,
and the action is a continuation of the other.
When Robert has entered, the one word
"Trouble" is sufficient to indicate to the
director that there will be a quarrel and
probably a fight.

The director will devise the action he
wishes to depict and will do it better than
you or I probably could, as he knows the
people in his cast and their various tem-
peraments. Directors make their own
troubles.

Of course in the scenario containing the
above scenes there were some preceding

scenes, showing Mary flirting at a party and then becoming engaged to Robert, but the scenes which I have taken at random from the scenario will clearly convey all that I intend, I am sure. I am trying to explain to you how simply and clearly scenes should be worked out, and that a great deal must be left to the intelligence of the director. Be concise in everything.

The scenario of a photoplay, which practically means the photoplay itself, is divided into a number of scenes, and every time the camera is shifted to a new position constitutes a separate scene; even though the camera is shifted back and forth to the same scene, after having been shifted to another position.

These are designated "cut-backs" or "flash-backs," when they occur after one intervening scene. Flash-backs denote very short scenes or flashes, and cut-backs typify reverting to scenes of ordinary length. The writer should not concern himself with the length of the ordinary scene he wishes to depict, as that will largely depend on how the director chooses to follow the action outlined in the script.

I have found that about 40 scenes to a
reel in a dramatic or melodramatic story is
what is most pleasing to the average producing director, and from 50 to 75 scenes
to a reel can be employed in the scenarioizing
of comedies; all depending on the quickness
or slowness of the action.

One of the chief points in good scenario
writing is to preserve a logical continuity.
By this we mean that the scenes and the
action of the story must run along in a
smooth sequence, without illogical jumps
and breaks.

Occasionally the continuity must be pre-
served by the careful use of "subtitles" and
"inserts," but these must be sparingly used
and avoided when possible. The less reading matter you impose on the screen, the
better. The employment of long, tedious
"subtitles" shows the hand of the ignorant
writer of photoplays. The public does not
like them, and the exhibitors hate them.
They prefer to pay for scenes and action,
and not for printed matter on their screens.

In working out your "continuity"—that
is, your scenes as they follow each other—
make a judicious use of "cut-backs" and

"flash backs," to create suspense and make the value of your main scenes duly felt. No scene should be too long. If the action of a scene is vitally important and threatens to be too prolonged, then break it up by flashing to some other scene, or insert a "close-up" or a letter or a worded "insert," and then flash back to the scene you have broken into. This will relieve the situation and make the interest centered in that scene more intense.

If your plot is a serious one and your photoplay aims to be a "thriller," you will find that you will get the thrilling effects you want by gradually working up to the crucial moments, and not rushing your

---

IF your plot is a serious one and your photoplay aims to be a thriller, you will find that you get the thrilling effects you want by gradually working up to the crucial moments, and not rushing your scenes too much. Create plenty of suspense.

---

scenes too much. To create plenty of suspense and keep the interest up to fever heat until the actual "thrill" occurs should be the main aim of the writer. Break into your main secenes with a series of "close-ups" and "cut-backs," particularly in cases where you wish to depict fights or hair-breadth escapes. The mere fact of two men having a quick tussle, in which one of them gets killed, does not necessarily constitute a thrilling episode; but if you can prolong the suspense for a while, giving the advantage first to one opponent and then to the other, and then make it appear that the ultimate winner is going to be the victim, but when all seems lost make him by a superhuman effort extricate himself and finally overcome the other—then you have probably got the audience worked up to the proper state of excitement, and you have landed the "punch" which is necessary to make the picture a success.

Then, no matter how serious the subject of your story may be, you should try, whenever possible, but without breaking the thread of the story, to inject some comedy touches, which will relieve the serious ten-

sion and keep the audience in good humor.
Stories that are too serious throughout are
apt to bore, and a touch of light comedy
injected now and then will always prove a
welcome relief. But do not let your comedy
be of the slapstick variety. Try and inject
some good comedy situations, which will not
altogether take from the serious plot of the
story, whilst winning a happy smile from
the audience.

The producing director will be quick to
recognize the comedy situation and will
gladly welcome it. If he is of opinion that
it is irrelevant to the story he will, of course,
eliminate it, but most directors are prone to
grasp anything that is likely to relieve a
production from monotony.

Film manufacturing companies are paying more careful attention to the cost of
their productions than they used to do.

Make your scenes short; do not elaborate;
don't try to be technical. Be clear and concise in the description of your scenes and of
your characters. Don't aim to be literary.
You are dealing with practical people
and you are aiming to do practical work.
For instance:—"Mary" is your heroine.

Describe her thus. (Mary;—Age 20—
Pretty.—Well dressed.) That describes
Mary. She is obviously wealthy, or she
would not be well dressed; that is to say,
"well dressed" as understood from the play-
wright's point of view; which is an opposite
term to "poorly dressed";—although, as we
know, many poor girls dress in better taste
than their wealthier sisters!

If a scene threatens to be unduly long,
then break it up, by either inserting a
"close-up" or a "cut-back."

I do not want any of our readers to get
the impression that I am aiming to *teach* the
art of photoplay writing, because I do not
believe that any mortal being can do that.
I am merely giving to others the experience
I have gained, and pointing out the pitfalls
which beset the unwary writer on all sides.

I must repeat to you again and again, to
go and watch the pictures on the screen, and
count the number of scenes in each picture
that you see. You will find that, on an
average, there will be from 40 to 45 scenes
to the reel in dramatic and melodramatic
stories; and from 55 to 75 scenes to the reel
in comedy-dramas and comedies.

Most of the best producing directors, who are affiliated with the leading film companies,—particularly with the feature producing companies,—employ two or three cameras in the filming of big, important scenes, and they are very wise in doing so, because they get results of uninterrupted "Action" that are not possible when using only one camera, which involves stopping the action in scenes in order to procure "close-up effects" or the same scenes taken (or "shot," as the technical term is) from different angles. I will endeavor to make this more clear, and show in a practical way what I mean.

Supposing you have a big ballroom or cabaret scene, in which you want to insert one or more "close-ups" of the leading characters, and you want to show the scene "shot" from different angles, so as to impart variety to the beautiful setting which the wise director will doubtless have prepared. Then the following is a very practical way in which to describe in your scenario the scene and the embodied "Action" which you want to convey.

Say your scene is number 63, a big ball-

room in which vital action connected with
your story takes place: then describe it like
this.

Scene 63—Big Ballroom, sumptuously furnished. Orchestra on balcony in rear. Glass
swinging doors, under the balcony, leading into
conservatory. Show Dick dancing with Rachel in
and out amongst the crowd of dancers. Ignatz
in foreground, looking angry and jealous. (Have
three cameras on this scene, shooting at different
angles, so as to get close-up of Dick and Rachel
dancing and enthralled with each other, and close-
up of Ignatz, his face distorted with jealous rage;
and also a focus on the door leading into conservatory, through which Dick and Rachel will go
together at close of dance, followed hotly by
Ignatz.) The action and length of scene and
number of inserts at discretion of the director.

Here you have the whole setting and
action of this dance depicted, all in one
scene, which can be carried out by the
director without stopping the action, thus
saving time; which is always valuable in the
filming of big scenes where high-salaried
artists and a number of extra persons are
employed. Besides, it will be more natural

and less strained than would be the case if the action were stopped every now and then to get the close-ups and the scene from the various angles. In fact, sometimes four cameras will be working on a scene of this character, one camera being stationed up in the roof of the studio, shooting down and getting a bird's-eye effect that is very pleasing.

I trust that I have made the foregoing sufficiently clear to the reader. The average director likes to have a scene described to him in this manner (I have learned by experience), and welcomes scenes such as this, because it gives his imagination full scope and condenses the action you mean to convey.

Never have unnecessary scenes in your scenario. If "Dick" is leaving his office to call on "Rachel," don't show him coming out from the office building, then going up the street, then entering the gate leading to Rachel's home, then ringing the door-bell. Just show him leaving his office, then cut to "Ignatz" drinking himself to death, or something equally exciting; and then cut to "Rachel" in the parlor of her home, a knock at the door, and Dick being admitted by the maid. Don't pad. Let the director do that, if he wants to; but don't *you* be guilty of padding, for it is a gross crime and lowers the standard of your play.

If you have a strong, gripping, one-reel story full of vital action right through, don't try and pad it out to a two-reeler. It will be weak then.

If you have a good, original story, work it out to its logical conclusion. Make every scene depict and *mean* something. Don't make your characters aimlessly walk about from one location to another merely to fill in scenes that can be left out of the production to its advantage. Nothing bores and irritates a moving picture audience so much as a "padded out" story, and if the moving picture industry is to continue to interest the masses a drastic embargo will have to be put upon needlessly-drawn-out film productions. If not, there will be a slump from which it never will recover.

The scenario writer is the responsible party of the first part and must avoid this above everything else. If there is a big slump in "pictures" the scenario writers will have to go back to fiction writing, or the banking business, or hog raising, or millinery, or whatever former avocation they found to be most congenial and profitable.

If your story calls for the depicting of vices, let it point a good moral and prove a warning to your fellow men and women that the cultivation of wrong-doing of any kind whatever does not pay. But your comedies must be absolutely clean and free from suggestiveness. Comedy and immoralilty make a very nauseating dish.·

What is the "technique" of a photoplay? I'm sugared if I know! All the wiseacres who are writing on the art of photoplay writing keep continually harping on that word, as if it were a mythical something that we grasp from nowhere, but which must be vitally essential to insure success. Bosh! To the Devil with technique! We want to be photoplay-writers, not technologists.

Of course there are certain forms to be observed in the construction of a scenario, such as making a short and comprehensive synopsis of the story—so short and closely knit together that the reader who has the power of accepting or rejecting the script may readily grasp the plot, without having to wade through a superfluous lot of matter that doesn't amount to a hill-of-beans. Then there's the cast of characters to be considered, with a short description of their ages, sex, and calling in life. (A few words devoted to each character is sufficient—such as, "Dick, a clerk, age 25, tall and handsome"—showing at once that Dick is a manly looking fellow, in humble circumstances, and therefore a hero!)

Then follows the working out of the scenes, and the shortest possible description of the action which is necessary for the producing director to follow. He will easily grasp what you mean to convey if you describe the action clearly and concisely. The following is a good example:

"Scene 6.—Parlor; Charley asleep in chair, his mouth open. Jane enters on tiptoe; tickles his nose with feather. He jumps up—she struggles—love scene—engaged—kiss—dissolve out the scene."

There! That's a long scene, with quite a deal of action, and any director who is not a fool can easily grasp the situation without having a lot of "technique" rubbed into him. Don't worry about technique—whatever it is—but keep your story in mind and make your scenes short and your sequence of them as logical and as free from "padding" as possible.

There is no mystery about writing photoplays. Anyone who makes a study of pictures on the screen and who can visualize a story and who can put that story into words which constitute short, crisp scenes, which will bring the story to a logical conclusion, can write a photoplay.

Every day more "close-ups" are being employed, and some directors insert them into nearly every scene, and there is no doubt

*B**E clear and concise in the description of your scenes and of your characters. Don't aim to be literary. You are dealing with practical people and you are aiming to do practical work. All scenario writers will be glad to know that the field is gradually broadening.*

that productions are being considerably improved by them, as they bring the audiences more in sympathy with the characters and make the portrayals more vivid. After all is said and done, we are dealing with photography, and every scenario writer should try and visualize his scenes with a "camera eye." I will even go so far as to say that every scenario writer should own a small camera and learn how to use it, so as to find out the limitations of the camera and how to employ it in shifting from one scene to another. Knowledge is always worth money, if employed in a practical way. Taking "snap-shots" will show you the value of "close-ups" in depicting the action of your scenes, besides giving you the knowledge of what can be embodied in a single scene through the eye of the lens, and what cannot.

In evolving your scenario you must pay great care and thought to the "continuity" of the scenes. You must visualize your story as you go along, and bear your characters in mind, as you would your pawns on the chess board, and never let yourself forget that a pawn may mean a king. You must always remember where each character is supposed to be, and where you have left him, or her, so that you can bring the character in easily when next wanted. Always create a logical reason for each character to be in each scene depicted. Don't have them wandering aimlessly about. And, above all, never have all your characters in the same scene. That is fatal.

Make two synopses of your story, and send them in together. One of them as short, concise and gripping as possible, so that the reader can grasp your plot in a twinkling; and the other more fully explanatory, going more into the detail of the story. And then, if the reader is interested in the plot which he has already quickly grasped, he will want to read the other, from which he (the reader may be a scenario editor or a director) will have to evolve the working scenario.

Always try and put yourself in the reader's place, and think what you would be inclined to do under similar circumstances. Wouldn't a good, short, concise, gripping synopsis appeal to you more readily than a long, formidable, uselessly explanatory bunch of closely-written sheets of reading

matter—if you had to read about fifty
photoplays a day? Which would have the
better chance of a sympathetic reading if
you were in the editorial chair?

A good title will often go far towards selling a scenario. The shorter the title, the better. One word will often be more potent than
four or five. Can anything be more descriptive than the single word, "HATE"? Or
the magic word "LOVE"? I am sure you
can easily recall many photoplay successes
in which the title was embodied in a single
word. "Deserted" and "Hypocrites" were
both big successes. A title need not necessarily be lurid, but it should be one easily
grasped and meaning something. A great
many photoplays are thrown aside without
even a cursory reading because the title has
not appealed to the readers or the scenario
editor. With a good, gripping title and a
fairly original plot, and with scenes clearly
described in logical sequence, a real scenario
will not go long a-begging these days.

In the little note-book which every scenario writer should always carry, several
pages should be reserved for titles, and
whenever one comes to mind that is worthy

of being recorded, it should instantly be jotted down. A title will often suggest a theme for a story and is almost as important as the story itself.

IV

MODEL SYNOPSES

I HAVE received many letters from Editors and Directors informing me that nearly all the photoplays submitted have synopses so complicated and long drawn out that the plots are difficult to follow, and take so long to unravel that the main points of the stories are lost. So, let me give this advice again: Make your synopsis as short as possible, and outline your story so clearly that a child can readily understand the main issues which you want to convey.

You should never localize your exterior scenes or try to describe them too carefully, because you cannot know in what city or locality the company which may produce your story is likely to be working at the time. If your story is a "Western" one, do not jump your principal characters to New York and show them in exterior scenes in that city. It would be too expensive a jump.

In cases where long distances have to be traversed and the action to take place in specified cities, then you should lay your scenes in interiors. Scenes laid in the country do not so much matter, because locations calling for parks, river banks, fields and country lanes and roads can generally be found that will pass muster for the localities intended.

Make your characters human. Bring them close to the camera, so that we can see their facial expressions and know what they are thinking about. If your characters know how to act and are anyway near the age they are supposed to be this can be accomplished with as much success as on the speaking stage.

What is more pitiable than a seasoned woman of 35 enacting the role of a kittenish maiden of 17, or of a stiff-kneed male thespian doing stunts for which he might have been forgiven in his early twenties (which to him are but a distant memory), but which now call only for ridicule, or worse? No, they may act until they are black in the face and until their wearied bones crack, but they cannot fool the camera!

Here is a model synopsis:

"WHAT HAPPENED TO JONES" — Adapted from
the famous comedy by George Broadhurst.
Produced in a five-reel feature film.

Ebenezer Goodly (a professor of anatomy), his
wife, two daughters and ward, Cissy, are expecting a visit from the professor's brother, the Bishop
of Ballarat, Australia. It is thirty years since
the professor has seen his brother, and none of the
family has ever met him. Secretly the Bishop
has been making love, by letter, to Alvina, an
elderly spinster, sister to the professor's wife.

The professor's youngest daughter is engaged
to Richard Heatherly, who is supposed to be a
very good young man. When leaving the professor's house, however, he drops a card of admission
to a prize fight. The professor finds it and ac-
cuses him. After much discussion Richard per-
suades the professor—"In the interests of science"
—to accompany him.

During the fight the police make a raid. Richard and the professor escape by crawling over a
stable and down a water spout. They are followed
by Jones, a traveling salesman.

A policeman was near enough to secure part of
his coat tail, but Jones gave him an uppercut and
got enough start to follow Richard and the professor into their house. He demands their pro-

tection, as "they are all in this." A new suit of clothes arrives for the expected Bishop, Jones seizes on them and is mistaken by the whole family for the Bishop. He thus temporarily evades the police. The real Bishop arrives. Jones and Richard get him to his room. Richard pretends to be a valet and when he is undressed, Richard bolts with his suit to insure temporary safety.

A note arrives from a neighboring sanitarium to say a lunatic wrapped in a blanket and imagining himself to be an Indian, has escaped. The Bishop, getting tired of imprisonment, also wraps himself in a blanket and comes down stairs. Every one thinks he is the lunatic.

The right one is, however, taken by the superintendent. The Bishop, finding Jones' torn suit under the bed, puts it on, and, being seen at the window by the police, is taken to the police station. He tells such a plausible story, however, that he is sent back again with the policeman for further inquiries.

The professor tells the truth (that the real Bishop in his brother). Jones, seeing the advantage, threatens to sue for $50,000 for false arrest of the Bishop, and the policeman begs them to let the matter drop and goes out crestfallen. Jones saves Richard and the professor from exposure by saying that he impersonated the Bishop to gain an introduction to Cissy, the professor's

ward, whom he has loved for a long time. Cissy,
who now knows the whole story, helps him out,
and everyone puts in a good word for Jones.

Here is another model synopsis:

Alphonse Marteau, a Frenchman, and his
daughter, Jeanette, live on ranch; his neighbor,
Franz Schmitt, German, and his son, live on adjoining ranch. Both Marteau and Schmitt are
veterans of the Franco-Prussian war of 1870.
They are good friends, though, and Max, son of
Schmitt, is suitor for Jeanette. Jeanette is knitting scarf for Schmitt's birthday.

News of the European war comes to both fami-
lies, bringing back to both men the memory of
their fighting, 44 years ago. Schmitt goes to
Marteau and finds the Tricolor on the staff before
his house; enters house and finds Marteau in old
uniform, covered with decorations; Marteau in
great excitement starts argument and gets insulting, finally striking Schmitt with his sword. Max
coming in with Jeanette, Marteau forbids Jeanette further friendship with Max; Max takes his
father home. There Schmitt orders Max to put
German flag on his staff and to get old German
uniform with the Iron Cross decoration. Max
refuses; Schmitt gets them himself.

Two weeks later. ˙ Schmitt recovered from Marteau's sword wound. Max meets Jeanette coinci-

dently on river where she is getting water; they plan to reconcile their parents. In the meanwhile Schmitt goes riding and finds Marteau unconscious, owing to a fallen log. Schmitt binds up Marteau's injured arm with scarf Jeanette made him, which he always wears. Schmitt places him across his horse; brings him to Marteau's home. Schmitt leaves Marteau in care of Jeanette.

When Marteau recovers consciousness, he recognizes Schmitt's scarf and feels remorse; he sends for Schmitt and Max and a reconciliation follows. A picture comes to both men's minds; both see themselves in their uniforms while between them stand Max and Jeanette, holding Stars and Stripes. So peace and contentment reigned in both hearts.

Moral: In a neutral country be neutral.

V

MODEL SCENARIOS

HERE is the model scenario of which the foregoing synopsis is the skeleton; it illustrates clearly the mode of expanding the synopsis into the working script.

CAST

Alphonse Marteau..............French farmer
Jeanette......................His daughter
Franz Schmitt.....German neighbor of Marteau
Max...............................His son
A mail carrier.

LEADER: *Subtitle 1. Peace and Friendship.*

Scene 1—Parlor in Schmitt's house. Schmitt on. Schmitt reading; Max enters with game; congratulates his father on birthday.

2—Exterior of Marteau's house. Marteau comes out; looks around; re-enters.

3—Parlor interior. Jeanette on. Marteau comes in, looking for Jeanette; finds her knitting scarf for Schmitt's birthday.

4—Close. Jeanette shows scarf to her father.

5—Parlor same as scene 3. Marteau and Jeanette leave room.

6—Exterior of Marteau's house, same as in 2. Marteau and Jeanette leave on horseback to see Schmitt and bring scarf and wishes to birthday.

7—Woods. Show Marteau and Jeanette riding.

8—Exterior of Schmitt's house. Marteau and Jeanette arrive; knock at door.

9—Parlor in Schmitt's house, same as in 1. Schmitt and Max on. Marteau and Jeanette enter, received joyfully; make merry; Jeanette puts scarf on Schmitt; joy and thanks; Max and Jeanette exit.

10—Schmitt's garden. Jeanette and Max caressing.

11—Garden. Schmitt and Marteau walking in garden.

12—Bench in garden. Max and Jeanette on, caressing; the two fathers come from behind bush and watch them delightedly; lovers walk out of scene; fathers shake hands.

Subtitle 2. Sad Tidings.

13—Schmitt's garden. Schmitt and son working in garden; mail carrier enters, bringing mail with news of European war.

14—Close. Show paper close, containing news about war between France and Germany.

15—Back to scene 13. Schmitt and son express regrets.

16—Schmitt's stable. Schmitt and son saddling horses to bring news to Marteau.

17—Fields. Schmitt and son riding.

18—Marteau's garden. Marteau on. Receives mail and news about the war; goes excitedly into the house.

19—Parlor. Jeanette on. Marteau enters excitedly; shows papers to daughter; Marteau takes flag from cupboard and both exit.

20—Exterior of Marteau's house. Marteau and Jeanette come out of house; Marteau starts to put up flag; Jeanette protests; no use; flag goes up.

21—Parlor, same as in 19. Jeanette enters, sobbing.

22—Road. Schmitt and son riding.

23—Parlor, same as 19. Jeanette on. Marteau enters in uniform with decorations, poses and flourishes sword.

Subtitle 3. Fighting Old Battles.

24—Garden. Jeanette on. Schmitt and son arrive and greet Jeanette; exchange news; Schmitt asks for Marteau; Schmitt goes towards house, while Max and Jeanette seat themselves on bench.

25—Window. Schmitt looking through window, sees——

26—Parlor. Marteau posing in uniform.

27—Window, same as 25. Schmitt looking into window; goes toward door.

28—Door. Schmitt knocks at door.

29—Parlor, same as 26. Marteau hears knock at door; goes to open door.

30—Door. Schmitt on. Marteau opens; Schmitt enters.

31—Parlor. Schmitt enters, offering Marteau hand in greeting; Marteau refuses; starts argument about war.

32—Bench in garden. Max and Jeanette kissing.

33—Parlor, same as 31. Marteau gets insulting.

34—Bench in garden, same as 32. Max and Jeanette hear noise in house; exit.

Subtitle 4. The Other Veteran of the Franco-Prussian War.

35—Parlor, same as 33. Marteau and Schmitt on; Schmitt wounded on head; Max and Jeanette enter; Marteau forbids Jeanette further friendship; Max and his father exit.

36—Room in Schmitt's 'house. Schmitt and son enter; Schmitt orders Max to take German flag from bureau and bring German uniform; Max protests; Schmitt gets flag himself.

37—Garden before Schmitt's house. Schmitt comes out from house and puts up German flag.

Subtitle 5. For the Fatherland.

38—Attic. Schmitt getting uniform from old trunk, lovingly.

39—Parlor in Schmitt's house. **Max** on. Schmitt enters with uniform and shows to son the single decoration, the Iron Cross, telling him about the war of 1870.

40—Close. The Iron Cross.

Subtitle 6. Lonely Hearts.

41—Mountain and woods. Max sitting on log; whittles stick; downcast; exits.

42—Mountain overlooking Marteau's farm. 'Max enters and looks to farm longingly.

43—Fade in Jeanette in her garden.

44—Back to scene 42. Max exits.

45—Bench in garden. Jeanette sitting on bench, lonely and dreaming.

46—Fade in scene 32.

47.—Back to scene 45. Jeanette kissing her ring and weeping.

Subtitle 7. Two Weeks Later.

48—Garden before Schmitt's house. Max cleaning fishing net; Schmitt comes and asks son to come with him hunting; Max refuses; Schmitt exits.

49—River. Max sitting by the river fishing. Jeanette appears on opposite side to get water.

50—Shows Max crossing river.

51—Other side of river. Jeanette on. Max comes through river; Jeanette falls weeping in his arms.

52—Close view of Max and Jeanette.

53—Back to scene 51. Max and Jeanette seated on rock; plan to make peace between their parents.

Subtitle 8. Anxious for News.

54—Parlor in Schmitt's house. Schmitt reading paper; happy over news of German victory.

55—Paper close; headlines, news of German victory.

56—Marteau's parlor. Marteau reading same paper; anger and disgust.

Subtitle 9. The Next Day.

57—Marteau's garden. Marteau reading paper; French repulsing Germans; shows happiness.

58—Paper close; headlines of French repulsing Germans.

59—Schmitt's parlor. Schmitt reading same paper; disgust.

Subtitle 10. The Accident.

60—Woods. Marteau busy with cutting tree; tree falls, striking head and pinning arm; unconscious.

61—Close view of Marteau pinned under log and still unconscious.

62—Woods. Schmitt riding; sees Marteau; hastens forward.

63—Woods, same as 60. Schmitt arrives; pushes tree back.

64—Close. Schmitt kneeling at Marteau's side; binds injured arm to splint with scarf.

65—Back to scene 60. Shows Schmitt taking Marteau on his horse and leading him to his home (Marteau's home).

Subtitle 11. Good for Evil.

66—Gate at Marteau's garden. Jeanette leaning on gate dejectedly; sees Schmitt approaching with Marteau over horse; Schmitt takes Marteau from horse and brings him into house.

67—Marteau's room. Schmitt and Jeanette bring Marteau in and lay him on couch; with kind words to Jeanette, Schmitt exits.

68—Close. Marteau recovers consciousness; recognizes Schmitt's scarf; is remorseful.

69—Back to scene 67. Jeanette enters; Marteau shows her scarf and tells her that Schmitt saved his life. Bids her to go and bring him; she exits.

Subtitle 12. Reconciliation.

70—Schmitt's garden. Schmitt and Max on; Jeanette arrives; asks them to come to her father.

71—Marteau's room, same as in 67. All enter Marteau's room; Marteau extends hand to Schmitt, which is gladly taken.

72—Vision. Marteau and Schmitt in uniforms; Jeanette and Max between them, holding stars and stripes.

73—Back to scene 71. Schmitt seated by Marteau's couch; Jeanette in Max's arms, kissing, etc. Happiness. Fade out.

Some Other Examples

HERE are two other examples of model photoplays, each with its synopsis, both synopses very short:

Enid and John Granger enter their home after the marriage ceremony, and on attempting his first embrace, Granger becomes aware of the intense dislike his bride has for him. Hurt and angry, he tells her that they shall be husband and wife in name only, and she passes into her room. There she goes over in her mind the manner of her engagement: When going to Granger to ask postponement of a card debt, he suggested his cancelling the debt or her marrying him to be settled by the turn of a card. They cut cards—she loses and their wedding is the result. He, going to his room, pictures to himself the card party at which she incurred the debt and at which her apparent liking for Gerald Stanley aroused his jealousy. Weeks later, when the guests at a garden party and dinner have departed, Gerald remains and is caught by Granger making love to Enid. Granger puts her out of room and offers Gerald a chance to win her by a pistol duel. Despairing of winning Enid's love, Granger removes cartridges from the gun he reserves for himself. Enid, seeing this, rushes in from hall and, dashing between them, bids Gerald go—declaring to the astonished Granger that it is he, her husband, she loves.

CAST

Enid Leroy.
John Granger.
Gerald Stanley.
Mrs. Carleton-Weed.
Guests, servants, etc.

PROPS.

Card Tables.　　Cards.　　Pistols.

SCENES

INTERIORS

1, 2, 3, 13 . . . . Boudoir, Enid's
4, 12 . . . . Bedroom
5, 6, 7, 8, 9, 10, 11,
　29, 31 . . . . Smoking room, Carleton-Weed
14, 16 . . . . Bedroom, John's

15 ....Drawing room, Carleton-Weed
23, 25, 27, 32, 34,
  36, 38, 39, 32A,
  33, 35.........Drawing room. Granger
24, 26, 37........Hall, Granger

EXTERIORS

17, 18, 19, 20, 21,
  22 ....Garden, marquee, pergola;
                Granger outfit
28, 30..........Another garden, showing one
                window of house

Scene 1—The first homecoming. Interior, boudoir, two doors at back. Enter Granger and Enid in bridal attire, preceded by butler, followed by maid. As Granger starts to help her off with her wraps she draws away from him in manifest dislike. He hands maid her wraps and maid exits. He starts to talk, but Enid is indifferent and stands with thoughts evidently far away. He takes her by the hands and leans over to kiss her, as if for the first time understanding her feelings toward him, he pauses, looks her straight in the eye, studies her for a moment. Her eyes do not falter.

Scene 2—Close-up picture of the two looking at each other.

Scene 3—Interior, boudoir. Granger slowly points to door, indicating that it is the door to

her room. Indicates that the other door belongs
to him. Registers that her room is hers and hers
alone. Opens the door and holds it open as she
passes through. Closes door.

Scene 4—Interior, darkened bedroom. Moonlight streaming in window. Enter Enid, and
standing in the moonlight, looks sadly out. Dissolve out.

Scene 5—Interior smoking room. Dissolve in
Granger drops to his chair as Enid enters. He
tries to look unconcerned as he asks what he can
do for her. He stands and places chair for her.
She refuses and seems in some embarrassment as
to how to begin. Granger looks at her with love
and anger struggling in his face. Finally Enid
gestures toward some cards on the table and gestures that she is unable to pay what she owes him.
Will he wait? He, too, looks at the cards, and
an idea strikes him. He takes up the cards and
begins to shuffle them, she looking anxiously on.
He looks sternly at her, and, cards in hand, gestures, cut in:

*"The best two out of three. If you win, I'll cancel
the debt. If I win you marry me."*

She starts back in horror, but he looks implaca-
ble as he awaits her assent. Suddenly the gam-
bler's instinct awakens, and with gleaming eyes
she gestures assent and eagerness to begin. He
puts the shuffled pack on the table and motions

her to cut. This she does. He motions her to take the first card. She does so and holds it till he has chosen. They hold up cards together. Hers the ace of diamonds, his the jack of the same suite.

Scene 6—Close-up of two hands holding cards.

Scene 7—Interior, smoking room. Discover the gleam of triumph in Enid's eyes. Granger looks perfectly calm and they each select another card. They show them to each other. This time Enid starts nervously. Granger maintains a stern calmness. Granger's card is the king of clubs; Enid's the queen of the same suite.

Scene 8—Close-up picture of two hands holding cards.

Scene 9—Interior, smoking room. Discover Enid now very nervous and Granger looking stern and calm as before. She hesitates before choosing. He takes his card at once. A look of frightened unbelief crosses her face as they compare cards. He holds the ace of hearts and she the ten of spades. Her hand trembles as she holds the card.

Scene 10—Close-up picture of two hands, hers trembling, holdings cards.

Scene 11—Interior, smoking room. Discover Enid and Granger as before. Slowly they put down cards and look in each other's eyes. He looks uncompromisingly at her, as with a gesture of pleading she begs to be let off. He gestures that she must keep to her bargain. Again she pleads, but he is inexorable and she turns to go. He reaches out his hand, which she ignores, and pulling herself together, exits with some degree oᵢ composure and dignity, after looking in freezing manner upon Granger, who looks triumphantly as exits. Dissolve out.

Scene 12—Interior, bedroom as scene 4. Dissolve in Enid coming back with a shudder. She turns and sinks slowly into chair; is convulsed with sobs.

Scene 13—Interior, boudoir. Discover Granger walking up and down, with angry look. He turns, looks at door of bedroom and exits.

Scene 14—Interior, darkened bedroom. Enter Granger, turns on light, closes door in angry fashion, crosses to chair and sits lost in angry thought. Dissolve out. (Interpose.)

Scene 15 — Interior, handsomely furnished drawing room of country house; card tables. Dissolve in guests just finishing an evening at bridge. Enid, John Granger and two others at table in foreground; others go up, leaving Enid and Granger in foreground. Enid indicates that she has lost. Gestures to John Granger that she will pay, but as she turns away, looks worried. He glances at her with a loving look, but as Gerald comes to her from Mrs. Carleton-Weed to whom he has been talking, and as Enid receives him with unfeigned joy, a jealous frown crossed Granger's face. Mrs. Weed circulates among her guests, most of whom gesture an intention of retiring for the night. Most of party exit through door to hall. Enid and Gerald exit, talking interestedly to each other. Granger follows, looking blackly at them and absently answering the remarks of his hostess, who walks to his side. Dissolve out. (Interpose.)

Scene 16 — Interior, bedroom. Dissolve in Granger, whose eyes gleam for a moment; sits looking moodily before him, then, rising heavily, goes to chiffonier and begins to take off collar and tie.

Their formal entertainments found her a perfect hostess and none guessed their strained relations.

Scene 17—Exterior, garden, marquee. Discover Enid and Granger receiving guests. Many other guests strolling about. Granger walks off with Mrs. Carleton-Weed and Enid talks to Gerald. They exit.

Scene 18—Exterior, garden. Enter Granger and Mrs. Weed; others enter and group talks.

Scene 19—Exterior, pergola. Enter Enid and Gerald, who is apparently talking lovingly to her. They seat themselves, and, he taking her hand, seems to be pleading, she only half reluctant to hear.

Scene 20—Exterior, garden as in 18. Group talking and laughing, as in scene 18. Granger, with a look about, detaches himself, and as he looks off his face grows angry.

Scene 21—Exterior, pergola, as in scene 19. Enid and Gerald as before, he apparently pleading and she not averse to listening.

Scene 22—Exterior, garden. With an angry gesture Granger is about to step off, when Mrs. Carleton-Weed turns and makes some laughing remark which causes him to return to group.

The last of the guests.

Scene 23—Interior, drawing room of Granger home. Guests of afternoon taking their leave. Gerald remains as Granger exits with Mrs. Carleton-Weed and party. Gerald goes over and takes her hand. He holds it as they talk. He presses her to elope.

Scene 24—Interior, hall and open entrance doors, curtained doorway to drawing room. Discover Granger standing at door, bowing to last of the departing guests. Butler enters from stoop and Granger turns away. Butler closes door and exits. Granger is about to re-enter parlor when he halts; stands horrified, looking through curtains.

Scene 25—Interior, drawing rooom. Discover

Enid and Gerald still hand in hand. Gerald looks about, then starts to kiss her. Granger's face is seen peering between curtains. As Gerald starts to kiss Enid he and she both sense the presence of some one, and drawing back, confront the stern face of Granger as he advances into room. As the embarrassed couple draw from each other Granger sternly gestures to Enid,

"Go to your room."

She exits with one pleading look as if begging him to spare Gerald.

Scene 26—Interior, hall, stairway. Enter Enid and starts upstairs, then changes her mind, and turning, listens in shamefaced way at curtains.

Scene 27—Interior, drawing room. Discover Granger returning from drawing curtains. He turns and speaks sternly to Gerald. Dissolve out.

Scene 28—Exterior, garden, window of house. Dissolve in Gerald waiting as Enid comes around corner of house. Gerald greets her warmly and she looks lovingly at him. Looking about to see if he is observed, Gerald kisses her hand. She only feebly remonstrates. Granger's face is seen at window.

Scene 29—Interior, smoking room, as before. Granger looking from window with angry and jealous look.

Scene 30—Exterior, garden. Enid gestures that she must go into house, and asks a question, gesturing toward house. Granger's face is hastily withdrawn as she looks up. Gerald gestures yes, and she exits with a wistful look backward.

Scene 31—Interior, smoking room. Granger walking from window with angry and jealous look and dropping into chair as door slowly opens. Dissolve out.

Scene 32—Interior, drawing room. Dissolve in Gerald beginning to look frightened and to glance about apprehensively. Granger goes to cabinet and from compartment takes out pistols. Going to Gerald he gestures. Cut in

"Only one man leaves this place alive, and he must swear to make Enid happy."

As Gerald turns shudderingly away, Granger gives a despairing look as though thinking of Enid. Then pulls himself together, and with a furtive look at Gerald and with an air of determination, deliberately removes cartridges from one of the pistols.

Scene 32A—Close-up of Granger removing cartridges. As he does this, Enid's face, with fear-widened eyes appears at curtains; gazes as if fascinated.

Scene 33—Close-up picture of Enid's face with fear-widened eyes, gazing as if fascinated.

Scene 34—Interior, drawing room. As Granger finishes he hands Gerald loaded gun, which he has to force on him as he protests in a cowardly way. Takes up broken and unloaded gun.

Scene 35—Close-up picture of Granger's hand picking up unloaded gun.

Scene 36—Interior, drawing room. At a signal from Granger, both men slowly raise guns and aim.

Scene 37—Exterior, hall. Enid draws back with an expression of horror; puts her hands before her eyes, then with a gesture of determination rushes from the hall.

Scene 38—Men about to fire as Enid bursts into room, and rushing between them, stands in front of the surprised Granger, looking at Granger with the eyes of a tigress protecting her young. Gerald's eyes drop; he lets gun fall to floor. Granger makes a move toward him, but Enid restrains him, and, pointing to Gerald, gestures, Go. He slinks out and Enid turns to the astonished Granger and gestures, cut in

"It's you I love, John."

He looks as if scarcely able to believe it. With a loving look she goes to him and he takes her unresisting into his arms.

Scene 39—Close-up picture of Granger taking the unresisting Enid into his arms.

Here is one of the briefest synopses on record.

Mr. Walter Greene, tiring of his wife's propensity for indulging in bridge parties and social functions, to the neglect of her domestic duties, undertakes to teach her a lesson, which is not without its effect.

CAST

Mr. Walter Greene.
His wife, Mrs. Greene.
Greene's father-in-law.
Greene's mother-in-law.
Greene's sister-in-law.
Latter's fiance.
Janitor of office building.
Female cook.
Butler.
Caterer.
Some bridge guests.   Women.

PROPS.

Cook Book. Novels. Fire. Cooking. Dinner. Tray of Food.

SCENES

1 ....Drawing room
2 ....Office

3 .... Ext. Greene's residence
4, 26.................. Hallway.
5, 8, 10, 16, 18, 20, 23, 25,
   28, 30.............. Parlor
6, 9, 12, 14, 22, 24, 29... Dining room
7, 11, 13, 19, 21, 27..... Kitchen
15 .... Ext. stationery store
17 ....Coal bin

Scene 1—Drawing room set. Animated party of women playing at bridge. Mrs. Greene, her mother and sister conspicuous. Game concludes with burst of hilarity as scene opens. Mrs. Greene, a heavy loser, rises, much chagrined. As the different ladies present consult the clock on the mantelpiece, more bustle is apparent. Good-byes are exchanged. Mrs. Greene takes tender leave of her mother and sister, after the others have gone, and then herself hurries out.

Scene 2—Office set. Late. Clock points to nearly six. Mr. Greene at desk, deeply immersed in voluminous pile of papers and letters. Entrance of the janitor with sweep awakens the man of business to the fact that it is time to think about going home. Heaving a sigh, he arranges papers in desk, refers to his watch, closes desk with tired, weary air, and with good-night to janitor, gets into overcoat and hat and hurries out.

Scene 3—Exterior Greene's residence. Nice-looking brownstone. Night. House dark and cheerless. Greene, hurrying along, stops, regards house moment, noticing desolate air about place, then taking out key, ascends stoop and admits himself. Taxi drives up. Mrs. Greene alights, pays driver and goes in house.

Scene 4—Hallway. Butler asleep. Greene enters and with disgusted air, arouses man, who jumps up and mumbles apologetically. Greene hears wife letting herself in, pauses moment, then disappears through door. Enter Mrs. Greene, who questions man as to whether her husband has come in yet. He replying in the affirmative, she also disappears through door already noticed.

Scene 5—Parlor of Greene home. Fire gone out; aspect of place cold and cheerless in the extreme. Greene comes in, notes the lay of things, calls butler, who enters hastily and sets about relighting fire. Mrs. Greene has entered almost immediately after her husband and has greeted him with a careless kiss. After which she hurries out, as she says, to dress for dinner. He looks after her a moment, his face grim and set, and goes out into the hall.

Scene 6—Dining room. No preparation for dinner visible. Greene enters, surveys table, looks vainly around for signs of food, and enters adjoining kitchen.

Scene 7—Kitchen. Cook, head on table, asleep.

No signs of a prospective supper anywhere apparent. Greene surveys the sleeping beauty for some time, then arouses her and tells her to get busy. Half asleep, she gets up, is profusely apologetic and sorry, and with a great appearance of bustle and haste, begins to get something ready.

Scene 8—Back to parlor. Greene re-enters, and his wife, resplendent in a dinner gown, sweeps into the room and immediately launches forth into a faithful recapitulation of the day's doings. Stops short in surprise as she notices her husband's unappreciative manner, but, putting it all down to a fit of sulks, shrugs her shoulders, looks at clock, and descends to dinner. Greene, after a moment's reflection and hesitation, follows.

Scene 9—Dining room again. Mrs. Greene comes in, seats herself and is served by the cook with some bilious-looking soup, which she does away with without question. Mr. G. enters, seats himself, is also served, partakes and pushes away the dish in disgust. His wife, noticing, demands to know the matter. He rises, dryly bestows a few encomiums upon the capabilities of the cook and his wife's ability to oversee the household in his absence, and quits the room. Mrs. G.'s first impulse is to rise up and follow him, but, rather indignant at his manner of speech, she thinks better of it and goes on with her meal.

Scene 10—Back to parlor again. Greene re-

enters and throws himself in a chair, inwardly
fuming at the state of affairs. Cogitates. Butler
enters and ushers in his father-in-law, mother-in-
law, sister-in-law and the latter's fiance, a saccha-
rine youth, all in evening dress. Greene responds
to their greetings distantly. They are surprised
to learn that he is not dressed for the evening, and
is not ready to accompany them, and ask impa-
tiently for his wife, who now runs in, breathless,
after a hasty meal. Mother and sister draw Mrs.
G. apart, and in muffled tones want to know the
matter. Mrs. G. shrugs her shoulders, remarks
that if her husband wants to be disagreeable, let
him; he'll get over it. Evinces a haste to be off.
All, accordingly, take leave of Greene and go out.
He thinks, takes out a cigar, smokes it, finds it of
little enjoyment on an empty stomach, throws it
away in grate, rises, paces up and down room.
Suddenly stops; faint smile passes over his face,
and striking the table energetically with his fist,
as though inspired with an idea, frames resolution
on the spot.

The next morning. Greene determines upon a
domestic revolution.

Scene 11—Kitchen again. Morning. Cook
sleepily preparing breakfast. Butler sitting in
chair, keeping her company, chatting idly. Door
opens quickly and Greene walks in, his manner full
of business. Butler jumps up quickly, surprised

and alarmed at such unwonted intrusion. Greene
ascertains just how far cook has progressed toward making breakfast, pulls out watch, replaces
it, takes out pocketbook, gives her money, tells
her briefly she can be off, much to the stupefaction
of cook, and goes through the same business with
the astonished and dismayed butler, and tells them
both the quicker they go, the better. Cook immediately drops what she is doing, bounces out, followed by the discomfited butler. Mrs. Greene, in
morning gown, appears in doorway, amazed and a
bit frightened at her husband's behavior. Husband turns to her, indicates that he will have no
more lazy cooks about, asks her peremptorily if
she can cook. She shakes her head, rather shame-
facedly, in the negative. Undaunted, Greene goes
to cupboard, extracts some eggs, pokes fire. Business of Greene cooking eggs stolidly. To allow
him time to do so, we can cut to

Scene 12—Dining room, as before. Mrs. Greene
comes in to sit and think, incidentally waxing indignant at her husband's unaccountable behavior
and at his audacious presumption in expecting her
to cook and attend house.

Scene 13—Kitchen again. Greene, having finished eggs and coffee, with which he has also had
some business, gets some plates and transfers eggs
to same and carries them in dining room.

Scene 14—Dining room. Mrs. Greene present.

Enter Greene with breakfast, his countenance passive and inflexible. Mrs. G., with touch of hauteur and offended dignity, demands an explanation of the morning's proceedings. He freezes her with chilly stare, meanwhile applying himself to eggs and coffee assiduously. She does not know what to make of the situation one way or another. Presently Greene finishes and rises. Mrs. G., rather awed at the stony silence which has prevailed through the meal, rises to kiss husband, hesitatingly. He responds icily and goes out. "What can have come over him?" she wonders, as she sinks down into' chair.

Evening. Further progress of the ˙revolution.

Scene 15—Exterior stationery store. Greene coming out, book in his hand, which he is glancing over, his face expressive of fixed determination and resolution. Close-up view of book, a cook book. He exits.

Scene 16—Parlor. Cheerless, empty, atmosphere as before. Enter Greene, stops on threshold, involuntarily shivers, looks angry. As he is wondering, Mrs. G. comes in with street wraps on, and greets her husband with decided air of aloofness, with which she has made up her mind to treat him for his conduct of the morning. She, too, is conscious of coldness and desolateness of the place. Greene removes coat, throws it on back of chair, and exits. His wife, puzzled, sinks into chair, wraps and all, and awaits his return.

Scene 17—Coal bin. Mr. G. descends into bin, fills scuttle of coal grimly, and reascends.

Scene 18—Parlor again. Greene returns with coal. Lights fire, his wife regarding him with an ironic little smile. Removes wraps and disappears for a few minutes, the while Greene has business with fire. She returns shortly with a novel, and ensconcing herself in chair, prepares to read, paying no attention to husband. Greene, having roused fire to some degree of warmth, exits in direction of dining room. Mrs. G. raises eyes from book and looks after him with curious interest.

Scene 19—Kitchen. Mr. Greene penetrates kitchen and, with fire in his eye, ascertains that the prospects for supper are of an extremely dubious nature. While he is standing, hesitating, there is a knock on the door. He opens it, to admit a caterer with supper. So astonished is the master of the house that he allows the man to push past him and deposit supper on table without interposing. But suddenly coming to his senses, stops the fellow, as he is leaving and questions him. "Yes, the Mistress' orders, sir." Mr. G.'s face grows dark. "Take it away," he orders, and he is obeyed with astonishment and rapidity. Mrs. G., whose curiosity has gotten the better of her, has followed her husband downstairs, and has entered in time to notice and comprehend what has transpired. Her breath comes in short, defiant gasps, as she surveys her husband. He returns the stare with such interest that she falters, and, turning, retreats, leaving him in complete possession of the field. He follows, bent upon carrying out his plan resolved upon the preceding evening. Scene 20—Parlor again. Mrs. Greene wavering between new-born fear of her husband and a defiant indignation at his course of proceeding, returns to her chair and ostensibly to her book. Greene enters, goes to overcoat, produces cook book from pocket, crosses to wife, asks her frigidly what she is reading. She does not reply. Gently but firmly he takes novel away and lays cook book in her hands. She looks at it, and rises, her eyes blazing with anger. He stands over her, ready for hostilities himself. She quails before the look in his eyes. In well-modulated accents, and with gestures to correspond, he informs her that he has made a tour of the kitchen and that the results of said exploration were anything but satisfactory, etc., etc. He further dryly observes that a diligent application to cook book which he has just handed her will go a long way towards the acquiring of that domestic tranquility and contentment so desirable in the home of all wedded young people. She sinks into chair, after apostrophizing

him as a bully, and tries to read the book, but
after little effort, tires of occupation and throws it
away pettishly to one side. Greene imperturbably
restores it to her lap, and then unable to control
herself further, suggests that she adjourn to the
kitchen and prepare supper. She rejects the
proposition with great scorn and a mocking laugh,
whereupon Greene takes her up in his arms, cook
book and all, and carries her out of room to
kitchen.

Scene 21—Kitchen again. Greene sets down his
frightened and amazed wife and placidly regards
her as he tells her to get supper ready. He doesn't
care what he eats, he says, but he wants to see her
cook something. He then takes up position before
door to prevent any possibility of her desiring to
retire, and watches. First he tells her she must
light the fire. Restraining her natural inclination
to sob, she goes through the business of lighting
the fire, and succeeds in burning her hand in the
operation. Forgetting her womanly dignity in
her pain, she runs to him, imploring sympathy,
entreating him to caress the injured member. Un-
moved, Greene extracts from his pocket a small
case, draws out a piece of court plaster and smacks
it on her finger and then, with heartless brutality,
sends her back to stove, over which she hovers
weeping, and commences with frequent reference
to the cook book, to prepare some mysterious con-

coction, glancing from time to time, at her relentless husband, whose face gradually takes on an expression indicative of satisfaction and triumph.

Greene's course of action has its personal disadvantages.

Scene **22**—Dining room again. Greene seated, wife seated, both eating, or trying to eat what Mrs. Greene has recently completed. Greene struggles to hide painful consequences of his heroic determination, while Mrs. Greene, who, despite her sore finger and sense of outraged pride, looks at her husband with an increased respect, also bravely endeavors to digest the mess for which she is responsible. Both finish, with visible relief. Mrs. Greene is about to rise from table and quit the room when a warning glance checks her, and she clears the table first, while her husband lights a cigar. This done, Mrs. G., without encountering any further opposition, prepares to go out. Greene calls her softly, and when she goes over to him, he kisses her quite tenderly, pats her cheek and resumes his seat and smokes reflectively. Mistaking the little affectionate demonstration for signs of weakness on his part and remorse of conscience, she calls him a coward and flings out of room. He does not resent the soft impeachment, but continues to smoke on in evident enjoyment.

Scene **23**—Parlor again. Mrs. G. enters, pauses undecided, hears doorbell, looks startled, goes out to answer, reappears almost instantly, followed by sister and her fiance. In tears, Mrs. G. relates what has happened, to the indignation and horror of her listeners, who comfort her, tell her to go upstairs and dress and they will await her. Reassured somewhat, she exits, leaving the worthy pair to discuss the matter exhaustively.

Scene 24—Dining room again. Greene, downstairs, has heard the bell ring and he is now discovered in a listening attitude. He smiles as the excited voices penetrate the dining room, and after a moment's reflection and temporary indecision he rises and goes out.

Scene 25—Parlor again. Sister and fiance warm over Mrs. Greene's treatment. Rise coldly as Greene enters and nods to them. Sister wants to know what his wife has done to be treated in such a contumelious fashion and is backed up, none too valorously, by her intended. Greene is about to reply in some heat, when his wife reappears in evening dress. Greene asks her quickly where she is going. She falters, with her sister. Greene, in decided accents, says she will stay at home tonight. Consternation, and a storm of objections. Greene, banging table fiercely, wants to know who's running the house. All look at each other in great alarm. Sister's courage fails her, and she remarks to her fiance that they had better go. He is quite agreeable, and sister, choking her emotion down and kissing the tearful wife, boldly declares Greene a brute, and hurriedly departs, followed no less precipitately by her bold escort, who can't get out quick enough. Left to themselves, Mrs. G. sobs for some time, and is ignored by her husband, who disappears for a moment, to return in smoking jacket. He lights pipe, and, taking up book, settles down for a comfortable evening. After Mrs. G. has wept herself dry, she steals several covert glances at her consort, which are not, it should be observed, without respect and even admiration, her face softens and she moves silently in his direction, as though she were inclined to make up. He looks up eagerly, expectantly, a trace of complacency in his expression, which she resents, whereupon she changes her mind, and, stamping her foot in a rage, retires.

Scene 26—Hallway, as before. Mrs. Greene rushes on, pauses, stands listening, a penitent look on her face. She disappears through hall.

Scene 27—Kitchen again. Mrs. Greene steals in, possesses herself of cook book and steals out.

Effects of the revolution.

Scene 28—Scene in parlor, as before. Mrs. Greene in evening gown, before cheery fire, reading book, two fingers swathed in bulging bandages, awaiting with impatience her husband's return from office. He comes in, and she throws arms about his neck. He is surprised and pleased both at his reception and the warmth and cozy atmosphere of the room. He returns his wife's kiss heartily. She takes off his overcoat, helps him on with his smoking jacket, which has been hung over chair in front of fire, and then taking him by arm, leads him off in direction of the dining room, to his ever-increasing delight and satisfaction.

Scene 29—Dining room again. Table all laid. Several choice viands conspicuous. Mr. and Mrs. G. enter. He regards table in admiration, and unable to wait, samples a bit of food right away. She admits with blush of charming confusion that she has cooked everything herself, holding up, as a proof, her two bulkily bandaged fingers, which he seizes and presses to his lips. They sit and eat and he marvels at the excellence of the cooking. She produces the old cook book and refers to its being the cause. "And you," she adds, hanging her head. He reaches over, upsetting a glass of water in his enthusiasm, and kisses her noisily. After which the meal progresses enjoyably.

Last stand of the enemy.

Scene 30—Parlor, as before. Husband and wife entering, are startled by ring at doorbell. He goes out and re-enters almost immediately, followed by father-in-law, mother-in-law, sister-in-law and the inevitable attending knight, all with their war toggery on. The former pair, in burst of righteous indignation, demand an explanation of

.the preceding evening's outrage, and hold their
welcoming arms out to her, expecting her to rush
into them and pour out the story of her agony in
sobs. But, to their astonishment and utter stupefaction, Greene's exultation and the bewilderment
of the younger people, who look particularly foolish, Mrs. G. gently expresses herself as having
been remiss in her wifely duties and that she has
discovered her mistake, etc. End up þy placing a
confiding hand in her husband's, whereupon Greene
looks stern and requests to know the meaning of
this unwarrantable intrusion, also, etc., etc. At
their wits' ends, the distracted parents faintly ask
their daughter if she does not wish to accompany
them out tonight. She shakes her head, a sweet no.
Father-in-law cautiously edges over to where
Greene is standing, and in a whispering query
wants to know "how he does it," but hearing his be-
loved wife call out in an awful voice, "Henry!" he
resumes all his former grandeur and pomposity of
manner and announces his readiness to retire.
Greene smiles to himself, and mamma, figuring
rightly that he is master of the situation, pleads
an excuse and sweeps haughtily from the room, followed by her faithful spouse, and the young people,
who say nothing, but content themselves with with-
ering the happy couple with scornful looks. Greene
sinks down into his easy chair with a satisfied
sigh. Mrs. G. seats herself on stool at his feet,

with a merry little laugh and lights his pipe, the pipe of peace. Dissolve picture.

FINIS.

VI

MANUSCRIPT PREPARATION

EVERY scenario must be typewritten. A hand-written script has about as much chance of being read;—let alone accepted;—as a lame mouse would have in a Cats' Home. We should always make a carbon copy; or better still, two; as the original may get lost and I have always found a carbon copy as efficacious as an original; although I have heard experts argue to the contrary.

Place your full name and address in the upper left hand corner of the title page of your MSS., and place a blank sheet of paper at the back of the MSS., thus ensuring that it may be kept clean, and worthy to be presented again and again, if it should prove unavailable to the first scenario departments to which you may submit it.

You must *always* enclose a stamped, self-addressed envelope with your scenario.

Do not enclose loose stamps, and expect the scenario department to supply the envelope for its return, if the manuscript is unavailable. The people in a busy scenario department have other things to do besides addressing envelopes. You must remember that you are submitting your scenario unsolicited and at your own risk, and that it is merely a courtesy on the part of the editor to return it to you at all. So, you should make it as convenient for him as possible. He probably receives a hundred photoplays a day, so try and put yourself in his place. If your manuscript gets lost or mislaid, you have no legal redress. However, if a stamped, addressed envelope is enclosed there will be little danger of that, as great care is taken in all reputable scenario departments to have manuscripts promptly returned to writers when these rules are complied with. But if you only enclose loose stamps, or, worse still, no stamps at all, then you deserve to lose your scenario. The chances are you will.

Do not write long letters to the scenario editors explaining that your story is gripping, or true, or original, or so full of heart-interest that the human pulse will quicken with fire on reading it. That will dub you a "Dub" and you don't want to be in that class. And if you are of the gentle sex, do not try to curry favor with the man in the editorial chair by informing him that this is your first effort at writing, but that you have real true violet eyes, and glorious lesliecarterian hair, and a perfect 36, and enclose a snapshot taken on the beach, by your best fellow, to prove it. It's a million to one the editor is a married man, and as such would not be in any way interested. I have seen such letters and snapshots received in scenario departments, and they invariably were passed around and caused much amusement, but the scenario, no matter how good, would never be considered seriously.

Let your scenario speak for itself. Submit it neatly typewritten, double-spaced, with a clean sheet back and front; your title on the outside front sheet, with your name and address in the upper left-hand corner, and altogether as neat and workmanlike as possible.

Every writer should learn to use a typewriter. I cannot too strongly advocate this. You can teach yourself. It requires practice; that is all. I know that for several years I labored assiduously with a pencil and gave out my efforts to be typed. It cost me considerably more money than I made in my first year of writing, and considerable time in correcting the mistakes of incompetent stenographers. I naturally tried to get the work done as cheaply as I could, and I *got* it. Cheap, but expensive in the end. I ultimately learned that one must do one's own typewriting, and you will soon learn that, too. Experience teaches. There is no other practical school.

I strongly advise writers to employ a

IF "a little learning is a dangerous thing," a lot of technique is a much more dangerous thing. Inasmuch as every studio has its own different sort of technique, why should you, a writer on the outside, bother your head about learning a universal technique? There isn't any.

---

black and red ribbon in typewriting their 'scripts; and to plant all subtitles and inserts of whatever nature in red, so that they will stand out clearly and will be easy for the directors to follow.

VII

KINDS OF STORIES TO WRITE

ONE-REEL comedy-dramas are nearly always in strong demand, and those with original plots and which hold a number of good comedy situations, will not go long a-begging. Remember, it is the situation that makes for real comedy and not foolish, childish acting, such as has been indulged in so freely in the past and of which the public has now become tired and disgusted.

Embarrassing situations from which there appears no means of escape always bring a laugh, and if the person embarrassed can extricate himself or herself from such a situation with ingenuity, then another laugh is provoked and the actor immediately gains the sympathy and good-will of the audience. Therefore, think up all such situations you possibly can and embody them in your comedy scenario. But in framing these situations bear in mind that the refined in humor is worth much more than the rough.

Never plant a "suggestive" situation in your comedy. Make it your aim and object to keep the moving picture screen as clean and healthful as possible.

Next to comedy-dramas good one-reel melodramas with a strong "heart interest" are mostly in demand, but they must not be too enervating or cast in too sordid surroundings. The public wants "thrills" and will gladly pay to get them, and the author who can provide them will find a ready market for his efforts.

But do not confine yourself entirely to one-reel melodramas. If your story is strong enough to carry itself into 70 scenes or more, then, by all means, work it out to its logical conclusion; but do not try to pad it out. Far better evolve a strong one-reel dramatic scenario, for which you will find an early acceptance, than to dilute your offering to a semblance of weakness. Watered stock is hard to sell.

Good "Western" dramas and comedies are always in demand, but should be submitted to companies who are working in a Western field. Leave "Costume" plays alone. The American public does not want them, and you must aim to give the public what it wants. Good American stories, with up-to-date costuming. That's what the public wants.

It is impossible to inform readers of the actual requirements of the various producing companies, because they are so apt to change in their policy every once in a while, and writers must take their chance in submitting scripts to one and the other, using all the discretion in their power. Every scenario writer has had to face the same difficulties with which you will have to contend, and the path of a writer is never an easy one, though it is always open to those who have the determination and the necessary gray-matter to stick to the thorny trail.

IF you know how to write a clever one-reel comedy-drama you need not fear that your manuscript will go a-begging. That is one of the most difficult of photoplays for the producing companies to get hold of, and they are ready to pay with liberality.

With brain and determination you can accomplish anything, but one without the other will only lead to a blind road.

Never attempt to depict allegorical visions, Scriptural visions or any visions whatever which savor of the unreal. Some directors have attempted them from time to time, with lamentable effects. Let them do it, if they will. Let them bear the ridicule that such things invariably invoke.

A chorus girl in a chiffon "nightie," with tinsel wings, a gilt wand and a halo, can never resemble a genuine angel, no matter how beautiful she may be. Leave "allegorical visions" alone, and stick to up-to-date, logical, practical, everyday happenings and facts in your writing of photoplays. Be human—and, above all, be clean and moral in everything to which you append your signature.

Never build a story on Biblical or historical events. The basis for such will not be reckoned original, and it is only for absolutely original subjects there is an outside market. All other sorts are handled by the staff-writers, and you do not want to waste your time, stamps, and paper.

Do not attempt to write "slapstick comedies;" they are invariably fixed up by the director who is producing that style of comedy, and, as a rule, do not need any definite plot. Besides, the so-called "Slapsticks" are getting out of favor. The public has been surfeited with them and they will soon, happily, disappear altogether.

Clean society comedy and drama are greatly in demand. The patrons of the moving picture theaters are growing tired of "Kitchen Settings" and "Regenerated Crooks,"—also of "Dying Mothers, Sick Children, and Drunken Fathers."

Avoid murders, suicides, burglaries, and other delightful crimes, even should you aim to make them teach a moral lesson by evolving dire and suitable punishments to fit them.

And above all, avoid everything questionable or immoral. The moving picture screen must be kept clean.

It is inadvisable to write on subjects of which you are not thoroughly conversant, or of peoples or countries with which you are unfamiliar.

Do not waste your time evolving "War

Stories." There is no demand for them. There is enough of them in the news-papers, and you can't beat realities.

Stick to American subjects. The United States is a big country and embraces every requirement in the way of atmosphere and types of peoples. Lay your scenes in the cities and localities with which you are familiar. Make your stories ring true. Did you ever see a single production made in the United States in which the scenes and characters were supposed to be European that wasn't the biggest kind of a joke? To those of us who have traveled, they are always pitiable, and on a par with the "Western-Cowboy-Indian" pictures pro-duced in France! Do you remember them? Weren't they delicious?

Photoplays intended for production in the Summer should be written and sub-mitted in the Spring; and should be mainly "exterior" scenes;—beaches, parks, and other pretty locations. Make use of the natural beauties of nature whenever pos-sible. Winter and Christmas stories should be submitted in the Fall, and in Winter stories you must depend largely on "in-

terior" studio settings;—for obvious reasons. Always figure in advance. To submit
a Summer story in August is waste of time
and energy, because by the time the story
would be under consideration for production it would most probably be October, and
the beautiful beach scenes you had so carefully arranged for would be impossible to
produce until the following Summer, and
no film producing companies contract for
stories so far ahead as that.

Do not try and evolve a photoplay from
any magazine story you may have read.
That is not playing the game, and there
will be certain to be others who are doing
it and the plot of the story will be hackneyed

*STAND guard over your plot if
you have an original one! Be
careful to whom you submit it. Do
not whisper it in confidence, even to
your best friend. An original plot
for a photoplay means big money
these days and gains in value every
day—if you market it first.*

before you have sent it in. There are too many writers doing that kind of thing, and that is one reason why some film producing companies are loath to accept photoplays from unknown writers. They may be purchasing the basis for a law suit, because the magazine writers and publishers are watching the film releases very closely now, in the hope of catching a stolen plot, and soaking a film producing company with good money at its back. That is one reason why staff writers and readers are employed.

The day of adaptations is rapidly passing, and the free-lance scenario writer is going to find an ever increasing market for his original photoplays.

No less an authority than Mr. W. E. Shallenberger, the able Vice-President of the Thanhouser Syndicate Corporation, and owner of numerous moving picture houses, has voiced his views on the matter in the daily press, and there is no man in the world better able to gauge the sentiment and demand of the paying public. He has announced in a public interview, as follows:

"I think that the conversion of plays written for the spoken drama and of books

written not to be visualized into multiple
reel features, but solely to be read, has been
overdone. Because I believe the motion picture industry is based on an art inherently
and absolutely distinct from the art of the
spoken drama or from the art of pantomime.
The really good screen play is the play written by trained screen play writers especially
for that most uncharitable thing in the
world, the motion picture camera. The
silent drama needs and deserves to have
highly trained and well paid specialists writing for it. They should be in step with big
affairs."

There is not the slightest doubt that in the
near future there will be an enormous demand for original scenarios especially written for film production. The public is
clamoring for logical stories, replete with
human interest and full of action and suspense. They want to see natural, beautiful
settings; fine, substantial stage settings,
and, above all, good, clean comedies that
do not depend on foolish acting or vulgarity
to win their favor.

VIII

SCENARIOS PRODUCERS WANT

IN the July (1916) issue Photoplay Magazine published letters from three noted scenario chiefs—Frank E. Woods of the Fine Arts Studio, Harry R. Durant of the Famous Players, and Colonel Jasper E. Brady of Vitagraph—telling what the companies do and do not want in scenarios and plays.

Mr. Frank E. Woods wrote:
"We have found, in this studio, comparatively little value in elaborately worked out motion picture plays, and for the practical purposes of our production we prefer narrative stories, unless the writer can be present during the preparation of the script for the picture.

"The writer of a motion picture play who is unaquainted with the studio conditions of the company to whom he has submitted his manuscript, is almost certain to involve his story in difficulties which are impossible to overcome if his manuscript should be followed, and if the best results are to be secured. Each studio, no matter where located, is subject to local and production conditions that differ from other studios. There are many things to consider of which the free lance picture story writer must be ignorant. The types of players to portray certain characters must be available; the settings or backgrounds may be impossible to secure, or may be far too expensive in one studio, while they might be cheaply had at others; the element of time in which the picture must be produced must sometimes enter into consideration; the peculiar capacity of the director to whom the picture is assigned, must be taken into question; in short these and other conditions are so numerous and important that when it comes to taking a script, no matter how well prepared by an expert author who has perhaps mailed it in from a distance, and turning it over to a director to produce, there at once arise necessities for making changes—and like knocking down ten-pins, one change in-

volves another, until the script becomes a
tangled skein of thread not easily unraveled.

"Of course there may be exceptions to
this general rule, but I cannot say that I
recall any in our experience here. Our best
success with outside writers who offer stories
to us for sale, and who are capable of preparing working scripts, has been when the
author could confer with the director and
our scenario and production departments
during the preparation of the manuscript.
In each of such cases the result has been
excellent. The author has been satisfied
and aided in the development of his story,
while the director has not been given the
opportunity or incentive to make any radical
changes, such as are often complained of
by motion picture playwrights.

"Although we have a considerable staff
of writers in our scenario department, we
are always desirous of securing good stories
from outside. If we buy so little, it is because out of the mass of material that is
being constantly offered we find so little
that is adaptable to our peculiar wants.
Everything we receive is carefully read, in
the hope of finding somewhere a diamond in

the rough; occasionally we find one, but not often.

"In order that photoplay writers may have a general idea of the character of stories we mostly desire, I will say that first they should consider the peculiar qualities of the stars attached to our studio. These stars and leading people at present are as follows: De Wolf Hopper, Douglas Fairbanks, Mae Marsh and Bobby Harron, Lillian Gish, Dorothy Gish and Owen Moore, Norma Talmadge, Wilfred Lucas, Tully Marshall, Seena Owen, Fay Tincher, Bessie Love, Olga Grey, and Constance Talmadge. Usually two or three of these players may appear in one picture. You will perceive

BREVITY, snap and clearness are the chief characteristics of the properly written photoplay synopsis, and not the least important of these three requirements is brevity. Remember that a scenario editor has to examine hundreds of manuscripts daily.

that the ingenue star predominates, and we are therefore always in need of stories in which the young girl is the principal character. Our requirements for Mr. Hopper and Mr. Fairbanks are quite obvious, as their peculiar qualifications are too well known to require explanation.

"The next point for the author to consider is the theme of the story. Each story should have an idea in it greater than merely an interesting series of events. It should have a central thought or purpose, not necessarily heavy. I do not think the public likes to think that it is being preached to, or obviously taught; these elements in a story should be incidental. Generally speaking, the author should endeavor to so construct his story that when the picture is shown on the screen it will cause the spectators to love or hate the characters as the case may be, and therefore care what may happen to them as the story unfolds. It has been my experience that tragic and depressing stories have no popular appeal, although they may be artistically superior.

"Historical or 'period' stories are not especially desirable, on account of the difficulties of costuming and settings. We might, however, accept stories that come under this class, if they have sufficient attractiveness; but as a general rule we prefer modern dramas, comedy dramas, or melodramas.

"One of the chief obstacles to the consideration of outside stories has been the idea among the authors who have submitted their material, that they must give us tremendous subjects that would require fortunes to produce. Owing to Mr. Griffith's great reputation—especially since his production of 'The Birth of a Nation'—a great many writers, among them some of the best in the country, are eager to duplicate that epoch-making motion picture. You can very well understand that such stories are scarcely ever possible for us to consider. It took Mr. Griffith more than a year from the time he decided to produce 'The Birth of a Nation' and commenced the preliminary preparation until it was finished. He has been at work on his present picture nearly a year and a half, and there is no reason to suppose that any picture he may make can be finished in less than a year's time. There

is only one **D. W.** Griffith—at least up to
the present time. And if there were another, and we had him among our staff of
directors, we could not produce pictures of
that character or quality in five reels and
on a weekly program. Mr. Griffith merely
supervises Fine Arts productions in a general
eral way. The actual work of the production itself must necessarily be in the
immediate hands of our staff of producing
directors, with the assistance and co-opera-
tion of our scenario and producing departments. While, therefore, we are glad to
have big subjects, we would caution writers
not to treat them in anything like the
magnificent way in which they would expect to see a 'Birth of a Nation' produced."

Mr. H. R. Durant of Famous Players:
"With interest in the motion picture increasing steadily, and particularly in the
motion picture plot and story, advice to
photoplay authors can be found in num-
berless newspapers and magazines, not to
mention those publications devoted ex-
clusively to the films. This advice, however, on the whole is general, and any plan

to give authors specific information as to the various markets for their wares should be of help not only to the author but to the motion picture manufacturer as well.

"Briefly, we are at present purchasing only ideas for five-reel feature pictures which are American in setting, which deal with modern characters and conditions, and which, above all, are original in theme and contain a big underlying proposition or motive, the whole cemented by a strong love interest. The leading role must suit one of our women stars—Mary Pickford, Marguerite Clark, Pauline Frederick, et cetera. Society and comedy dramas are particularly desired.

"Writing a five-reel feature is not, by any means, a simple task. You will more readily realize this fact when you stop to consider that the film of a five-reeler is approximately one mile in length, contains from one hundred and fifty to two hundred and fifty scenes, and consumes one hour and fifteen minutes on the screen.

"In other words, the plot must be replete with entertaining situations, the characters must be human beings, and the suspense and denouement must be so handled by the action that the audience will be interested up to the last foot of film. Merely a series of incidents or episodes in the life of a character or group of characters is not enough. There must be a logical progression of events leading up to the one big climax of the picture.

"Strange as it may seem, fully seventy-five per cent. of the successful novels as written are unsuitable for feature material. Why? Mainly because they do not contain sufficient action. And for this reason fiction authors of wide reputation fail continually as photoplay authors—they do not understand that words and atmosphere, charac-

BEING logical is one of the most important virtues in the photoplaywriting field. The public is generally shrewd. What Barnum said about its liking to be fooled is growing rapidly less true. An illogical plot is an imposition, and impositions are boomerangs.

terization and description, do not spell
screen action.

"In writing a five-reel feature plot very
much the same procedure might be employed
as in planning a five-part magazine serial.
Magazine editors and authors know the
importance of the 'curtain' at the end of
each instalment—the dramatic scene split in
two, followed by the usual 'To Be Continued' notice, which rouses the interest and
curiosity of the reader to the extent of purchasing the next issue—and authors should
recognize the equal importance of big scenes
and situations in the picture plot. Conflict,
struggle, tense moments, amusing incidents
to relieve the monotony—that is what the
picture-goer wants to see in the neighborhood 'movie' theatre, and that is what we
have to supply.

"What sort of material do we *not* want?
you ask.

"We are not interested in stories dealing
in any way with war—the public has been
surfeited with this phase of history through
the newspapers. Nor are we buying ideas
which have to do with labor problems, poli-
tics, or dual roles. We are not in the mar-

ket for costume plays or plots which are
foreign as to locale, atmosphere and characters. We do not desire ideas in which drugs,
liquor or vice play a conspicuous part; and
at the present writing we are not buying
stories calling for male stars. Plots which
have an unpleasant ending do not appeal to
us. The faith of the world is that *everything*
is going to come out all right in the end;
so why not stick to this theory in the motion
picture?

"Now as regards the form in which to
submit material: Do *not* send us complete
working scripts of your plots—that is, the
technical scenario which maps out the action
scene by scene. All we ask for is a detailed
synopsis, two or three thousand words in
length, outlining the story. Our working
scenarios are prepared in our own office by
masters in this art, for experience has taught
us that scripts from the average photoplaywright, who knows little or nothing of studio
conditions and the limitations of the camera,
are worthless as such. Also, please do not
submit plays, books or complete manuscripts
of novels or novelettes, as we have not the
time to wade through them. Send us only

synopses, and if we are then interested, we may ask for the play or book, provided the story exists in either of these forms.

"Unavailable ideas are usually returned within a week after their receipt, but occasionally we become deluged with scripts and are unable to adhere to this plan. Plots which have possibilities are held for further consideration. In any event, we do our best to render decisions within a fortnight at the latest, and we pay the market price immediately upon acceptance.

"Authors should know that familiarity with the scenario market is half of the photoplaywright's game. To mail scripts blindly to the film manufacturers, regardless of their requirements, is the height of foolishness. While you are peddling your plot at random, a wiser scenario author may be writing the same general idea for some particular market, with the result that he beats you to it and your plot is rendered worthless.

"You can't sell a mowing machine to a butcher, nor a single-reel picture to a company that produces only five-reel features. Watch the trade publications and learn the specific needs of the film manufacturers. Then offer your goods to the proper market and you are certain to get results, provided, of course, your stuff is salable.

"In conclusion, writers should know that if an idea will not make a good novel of 70,000 words or a good four-act play for the legitimate stage when worked out properly, the same idea is *not big enough* for a five-reel photoplay. This is an important thing to consider. That authors are not considering it is evidenced by the fact that out of the mass of material which is submitted to us we purchase only *one-half of one per cent!*"

Colonel Jasper Ewing Brady wrote:
"The Vitagraph is in the market for good one-reel comedies, and three, four and five-reel dramas. We do not want costume stuff, and a military play would have to be of sterling worth to get a hearing. If the various authors and would-be authors would send a commonsense synopsis with their scripts they would get a great deal quicker consideration.

"I make it a point never to hold a script longer than a week at the most. I know

this has not always been the case, but it is
now and will continue as long as I am in
charge of the scenario department. My
theory is that an author honors us when he
or she sends us a script. Perhaps their living depends on their writings. If that is so,
it is but right that they should have prompt
action, either for or against. I think you
will find that the day has gone by when a
company can hold a script as long as it
pleases and pay for it when it pleases. Good
scripts are too scarce to have any foolishness along these lines.

"Comedies are the hardest things to get—
good, bright one reelers with a story running through their foolery. I want stuff

*TIME was, not long ago, when
producing directors paid almost
no attention to the actual cost of
filming a photoplay. That time has
passed. The relation between production cost and probable profits is
being more carefully scrutinized
daily. Bear this in mind.*

for Frank Daniels, Billy Dangman and Hughie Mack, and the Vitagraph will pay well for it.

"Some days we receive as high as three and four hundred scripts, and many times not one is found acceptable. After a big murder case or some startling crime the mails are overburdened with scripts dealing with it in every conceivable form. I wonder if the public do not realize we are onto our jobs, and that our staff writers are looking for such things?

"The necessity for the trained scenario writer is here—but he has not reached the top of his earning power. That time is coming—and coming with the speed of a prairie fire—which, you will admit, is some speed. It takes a peculiar combination to make a good scenario writer, and few have the necessary qualifications."

Of intense interest to writers of scenarios is an announcement made by Jesse L. Lasky of a new departure by the Lasky Feature Play Company in the examination of manuscripts submitted.

Mr. Lasky's announcement is in the

nature of a heavy-artillery answer to all those who have attacked and criticised his recent and widely circulated article to the effect that the art of motion-picture producing was not advancing, because of the failure of novelists, dramatists and scenarioists to provide good stories for filming.

Now Mr. Lasky comes out with the announcement that he has established a scenario department intended to do away with as many as possible of the evils existing between authors and producers. Briefly, Mr. Lasky promises:

1. That all material submitted will get quick consideration and if not acceptable will be returned to the author with "a very carefully written constructive criticism" pointing out the reasons why the story was not worth purchasing.

2. If the story contains an idea worth developing, Lasky agrees to collaborate with the author for its development into such form as will justify Lasky in paying a good price for it.

3. Hector Turnbull, formerly dramatic critic on the New York Tribune, has been engaged to head the new scenario depart-

ment and to devote all of his time to encouraging and assisting authors.

4. Lasky is ready to pay well for ideas submitted in synopsis form.

If authors will respond to this proposal as earnestly as Mr. Lasky has made it, if looks as though the sun ought to shine 365 days in the year in at least one sector of the scenario horizon.

IX

MAKING THE GAME PAY

NOW, all free-lance scenario writers, besides being anxious to gain all knowledge they can of technique and the proper form in which to submit their plays, are also vitally interested in learning the best and easiest way of marketing them. There is no easy way. There are hundreds of thousands of people writing photoplays, and there is a very limited market.

If you have been lured by "The Call of the Pen," do not be discouraged if your initial efforts have not been crowned with success. They seldom are. But the need for good photoplays is growing stronger every day, and it is worth your while to bend all your energies to perfect yourself in the writing of them. Don't waste your spare time. An hour or two spent in front of your typewriter, with your thinking-cap on, may eventually land you in a pleasant and lucra-

tive position. It has for others. Why not
for you?

They claim all around that the film companies are finding it more difficult every day
to procure good original photoplays.

I don't suppose the free-lance writers who
are having their scenarios steadily rejected
will agree with them in this. And the free-
lance writers are right. They represent the
big mass of the people who patronize the
moving picture theatres and who study the
pictures on the screen, and if more serious
attention were paid to them by the real heads
of the film-producing companies more original stories would be the result.

At the present, as in the past, there are
too many producing organizations in which
the directors have it all their own way, and
are either writing the majority of the stories
themselves—glorying in seeing their own
names on the screen both as authors and
directors—or else are having the stories written by their office or neighborhood intimates,
wofully ignoring the fact that neither they
nor their friends possess any novel idea or
original plot, or are in the slightest way
qualified to deal with the amazing subjects

they frequently choose. I make this statement deliberately, at the same time bearing in mind the very few producers who are encouraging a new school of authors, and the few others who are endeavoring to screen reputable stage dramas. These worthy manufacturers are, I regret to say, sadly in the minority, and in company after company the authority-drunk director is grinding out his vapid, worthless plays like so much link-sausage!

The scenario editors and staff-writers cannot raise their voices in protest, because they have to kow-tow to the directors. If they did not hold the good will of the directors they would not hold their positions for any length of time. This state of affairs has continued since the inception of film productions, and with all that has been written on the subject the real state of affairs has not been voiced by writers on the scenario staffs.

All this, you may say, is irrelevant to "Hints on Photoplay Writing," but I have received so many wails from disgruntled scenario writers who complain that there appears to be such a small demand for original photoplays, that I feel it to be my honest duty to encourage them not to throw up the sponge. The motion picture industry is going through a certain phase, that is all,—a mere "try-out" of something new, for which some manufacturers are paying heavily, and is, therefore, bound to be short lived.

I had one one-reel comedy that I submitted twenty-six times—to every scenario department in the country—and which was eventually accepted by an editor to whom I had already submitted it twice; but bless his hard old heart, he never knew that. The third time he got it, it probably happened to be timely. So, you never can tell what may happen in this writing game. Take it seriously; look upon it as a legitimate industry.

Every writer who can evolve a good original plot should work that plot into a magazine story and submit it for publication. Scenario writing and magazine writing should go hand in hand, and one will assist the other.

Many will claim that although they can write a photoplay, they cannot possibly write their original plot into a story which might prove interesting to the editor of a popular magazine. In nine cases out of ten it is pure laziness which holds the writer back from making the effort. Well, that laziness must be fought.

If one has a fair education and the ability to write at all, then why not put one's whole energies into the game? The photoplay is with us and is going to prove a lucrative field for many thousands who are as yet unknown to the public who are making and will continue to make moving pictures their chief form of amusement, so why leave any stone unturned that may lead to fame and fortune?

---

*P*HOTOPLAYS *intended for production in the S u m m e r should be written and submitted in the Spring. Winter and Christmas stories should be submitted in the Fall. Always figure in advance. Do not try to evolve a photoplay from any magazine story you have read.*

And then, besides, there is a certain
charm to the writer in evolving an original
plot into a well constructed story. The
interchange of dialogue between the characters gives them life and individuality,
which it is not possible to impart to them
in a scenario, no matter how vivid and
virile it may be. And besides the pleasure
which a writer experiences in seeing the
story between the covers of a magazine, and
the satisfaction of work well done, there is
the much better chance of finding a market
for the scenario which is based on the published story. Most of the scenario writers
who have gained any sort of success have
been contributors to magazines or news-
papers, or the authors of books.

On the other hand, there are many writers
who have scored big successes in the magazine field who have, as yet, not turned their
attentions to the photoplay, but their numbers are growing daily less. They are beginning to find the photoplay an extra scope
for their talents, and their brilliant names
are lending added dignity to the screen.

This will necessarily make it incumbent
on the scenario writers to bend to more

earnest efforts, as they must now compete with the men and women of tried ability, many of whose names are household words, and whose signature to a photoplay is recognized as a hall mark of competence. But this should not deter those who are blest with ambition, for the scenario field is a wide and open one.

Above all, do not be discouraged. The day of the original scenario is coming back, and the plots that you have treasured may be worth their weight in gold.

Do not be disgruntled and discouraged if your initial efforts do not meet with success. Do not bear a grudge against the scenario editors or the producing directors if they do not think as highly of your work as you do yourself. They may not be able to write as good a photoplay as you, but they are probably better judges of what they require than you can possibly be. A hen lays a good egg, but you would rather trust to your own judgment than to hers in passing on the merits of an omelet!

Always submit your photoplays direct to the scenario editors. If you have an original scenario which has an original plot, do not place it in the hands of any party who may advertise to sell photoplays, no matter how alluring the advertisement or how honest it may seem. If you do, you will be the biggest kind of a fool.

You cannot copyright a photoplay scenario. Many writers make anxious inquiries on this point. The only way to do so would be to tell your story in fiction or in verse and have it printed,—an expensive process.

But even if one could copyright a photoplay scenario, it would be of little use, because it would be very easy to change the title and slightly alter the plot, and the original author would find it very difficult to establish the fact that it had been pur-

---

IF you have worked out a good, practical scenario with an original plot, you are certain to find a market for it sooner or later. The scenario editor to whom you submitted it six months ago may be more than glad to consider it now. You never can tell what may happen.

---

loined. However, writers need have little fear on this score, because scenario editors are honorable men and they would not hold responsible positions for any length of time if they deviated from the ethical path.

Staff-writers should not be allowed to read 'scripts submitted by free-lance writers. I have always contended this. "Readers" should be employed for this purpose, and they are being so employed, now, by the best of the film companies.

The various methods of the various companies and their various producing directors should be closely studied, and the only way for the free-lance writer to get a line on their work is by a close study of their efforts on the screen. Go and see all the short reel pictures that you can.

The study of long so-called "feature" productions will not help you very much, because they are beyond your market. Features are written by the staff-writers or the directors themselves, and are always planned in the studios beforehand. Except a free-lance writer is especially requested to write one, she or he is only wasting time and good paper. No matter how good your long five

or six-reeler may be, if you are not well
known you will find it almost impossible to
find a market for it. If a day laborer tried
to sell a genuine $20 gold piece in Wall
Street for $15 you can imagine the slim
chance he would have of disposing of it! It
would be dubbed a "gold-brick," no matter
how good or new it might be. Well, your
long, laboriously worked out feature would
be in similar case. The Wall Street wiseacres often get stung by what they consider
sure-fire propositions, but, more often than
not, they will blame the state of the market,
and not the real cause of the flivver. The
real heads of the film companies rarely take
the trouble to go into the matter of the
scenario—they are too busy!

When you study pictures on the screen
you should make note of the name of the
producing companies and also of the directors, and try and gauge the class of stories
which seem to mostly appeal to them. You
should also count the number of scenes in
each picture, and jot it all down in a note-
book, which you should carry for that purpose. Become for a time a picture "fan."
You will learn more from watching pic-

tures on the screen than is possible to be obtained from any book or treatise on scenario writing.

If it is your intention to write magazine stories and to evolve your stories from your scenario plots, then it is advisable to reserve the fiction rights, and to state the fact on the front cover of your photoplay. Scenario editors will not object to your doing this, and will reserve to you the option of writing your own plot into a fiction story and reaping the financial reward. Otherwise your photoplay may be worked into a fiction story by some hack writer, and—from your point of view—hopelessly mishandled.

I also strongly advise magazine writers to reserve the moving picture rights to their stories when submitting them to editors of publications; otherwise they will debar themselves from reaping the benefits which should rightfully belong to them. I have always done so, and I have never regretted doing so. Safeguard your own interests as well as you can, because no one is going to help you in the same way as you can help yourself.

You should never attempt to sell a photo-

play unless you are fairly well convinced
that you have a salable article. Don't waste
stamps. Remember that the average scenario department receives on an average from
100 to 150 scripts daily, and 99 per cent of
them go into the waste-paper basket. Don't
feed that surfeited adjunct of the Editor's
office. Be satisfied in your own mind
that you have a story that is original, and
that it is worked out in intelligible fashion,
with continuity of action which will carry it
right along to a logical conclusion. Visualize every scene carefully and try to depict
in your mind's eye how it would appear to
you on the screen. When you have all this
well established within your thinking-booth,
then typewrite it, or have it typewritten, and
consider which company it would be most
likely to appeal to, and send it on its
journey, with a self-addressed envelope,
stamped, in accordance with regulations,
and await results. You will probably be
agreeably surprised.

To such of you who have stories that have
been rejected, and which you have long
since despaired of being able to dispose of
to advantage, I strongly advise that you dig

them up from the bottom of the trunk, and look them carefully over. You may find that the stories are still original, and only need a little revision. Typewrite them afresh, so that they will not appear to be shop-worn. Musty fruits don't sell.

You may claim that I am optimistic; but I am not unduly so. I am in a position to know; and I can assure you, my readers and fellow scribes, that the real heads of the various film producing companies are beginning to sit up and take notice, and are finding out, at last, that the STORY is the corner stone of the photoplay production into which they are sinking their own and their stockholders' money.

ORIGINALITY is the worcestershire of the screen. Don't waste your time trying to sell stale stuff. Stale stuff is as easy to get as orange culls in California. Better mail out any day a crude but plotty original story than the most polished of stale stuff!

Stories are not, as formerly, being purchased wholesale, to be buried away in scenario departments on the chance of their being some day selected by one of the directors for production; and no material is now being negotiated for unless it has been absolutely decided that it is going to be of practical use.

That is one of the main reasons why fewer stories are purchased from free-lance writers than was formerly the case. But this state of affairs will soon be changed. Fresh, original ideas and plots are sadly needed in the film business, and the directors have fully demonstrated that they are not capable of producing them. The staff-writers cannot be expected to supply all the original stories required; that is demanding too much of them. They are, for the most part, practical scenario writers, and must be employed to whip the ideas of the free-lance writers into such shape as to make them easy for the directors to handle. Each department has its particular use.

The average director has more than his hands full in looking after the production of a story, without having the task of thinking out and evolving the story himself. There is no use in arguing that fact. We see their efforts every day on the screen, and if they want to keep the theatre-going public interested in moving pictures, if they desire to preserve the goose that lays their golden egg, they will leave the writing of the stories to the men and women who have new and virile ideas.

All this is a preamble to the fact that there is an ever-increasing demand for the efforts of the free-lance writers. Their stories have long been wilfully kept back, through the selfish motives of others in salaried positions, until hundreds of these writers—many of them with big plots and ideas which would put big money into the coffers of the film-producing companies—have grown discouraged and have discontinued their worthy efforts in disgust.

There is an urgent demand for their big ideas, but the writers are groping in the dark. They feel themselves helpless. They do not know to whom to turn for advice as to the best means of having their good stories even seriously considered by the men in real authority. In their distress many of the sterling writers in the country have placed their stories in the hands of the petty grafters who advertise in various publications that they are in touch with the film companies and in a position to sell their stories for them. Advertisers who claim to be able to teach successful scenario writing, and who assure their innocent victims of a market for their stories, should be made the subject of inquiry by the United States postal authorities. Anyone who aids palpable frauds on the gullible innocents of the public is equally guilty, and should be swiftly brought to book.

Believe me when I say that if a writer cannot sell a story direct to a film company, there is no one who can help that writer to do so. Some of these advertising gentry claim to have been scenario editors and staff-writers and to be experts in their line. But if they were capable of writing as good a story as you are yourself, they would be busy selling their own stories, not yours.

That is evident on the face of it. Writers who are worth their salt are too busy turning their own ideas into practical use to bother with the efforts of others. You will find that it is usually the incompetents who advertise that they are competent to teach subjects which *cannot be taught*. No one can teach scenario writing. Only a close study of the pictures on the screen can do that, along with an education which enables you to string your ideas into a concrete form that can be readily understood by an intelligent reader. If a good housewife is expert at making home jam or preserves, she will not advertise to teach the other housewives around her neighborhood how she does it. Not on your life! She is too busy making jam and preserves, and too much of an expert to be a petty grafter.

I have given the hint before that every

---

*Y*OU *cannot copyright a photoplay scenario. Many writers make anxious inquiries on this point. However, writers need have little fear on this score, because scenario editors are honorable men and would not hold responsible positions if they deviated from the ethical path.*

---

writer who has an original plot worthy to
be evolved into a photoplay should also write
his or her plot and ideas into a fiction story
and submit it to the magazines to which the
story would be most likely to appeal for
publication. If you are going to take up
the business of writing at all, go in for all it
is worth. Don't be a piker. Don't be a lazy
writer. One form of literature will help the
other, and there is a bigger field for the
writer of short fiction than there ever was
or ever will be for the scenario writer.
Don't have all your eggs in one basket. No
writer can gain a literary reputation worth
while by solely writing photoplays, and if
you are seriously going to take up a literary
career at all you should study the business
from all angles.

A caterer who is running a restaurant
would never dream of offering only soup
to his patrons, no matter how good his soup
might be;—no, he offers them good, sterling roasts and stews; and other delectables
as well;—he goes the limit. The writer
should also go the literary limit. Put all
your talents to work. Some of them may
be latent, or dormant. Wake them up, for

we all want to sell scenarios, and to get the best price possible for them. Most of the best companies are paying better prices than they did formerly. Twenty-five dollars per reel was, up to a year ago, the usual price paid for the average scenario. Few of the higher class companies now pay less than $35 for scripts from unknown writers, and most of the well known scenario authors are demanding and getting from $100 to $200 per reel for original stories, and from $75 to $150 per reel for adaptations from stage plays and books.

Everyone who intends to take up writing as a means of livelihood, of which photoplay writing is now an important side issue,

*I*F the author of an original photoplay were given the credit and publicity which are his due, film productions would be considerably improved. The scenario writers would put more heart and soul into their work. Not all directors are guilty of this crime.

should perfect herself or himself in all the essential details connected with the chosen calling. The carpenter makes a confidential study of the saw, the hammer, the chisel, and his other essential tools, and would not consider himself competent if he could not use them effectively. Then, why should a writer be deficient in the knowledge of how to use the very simplest and absolutely essential tools of *his* trade? Why should the writer be dependent on someone else to do the necessary work?

A great number of photoplay writers have, I know, become greatly discouraged by lack of recognition, and by having their worthy efforts returned again and again by all the companies to whom they have been submitted; but I am making no idle prophecy when I assure all creators of scenarios that every original story that has been ruthlessly spurned in the past will soon be grabbed at, if reconstructed to meet modern methods of direction and production.

ADDENDUM

DIRECTORY OF PRODUCING COMPANIES

F OR the benefit of scenario writers Photoplay Magazine publishes monthly a list of the chief film-producing companies. This is the list:

STUDIO DIRECTORY

For the convenience of our readers who may desire the addresses of film companies we give the principal ones below. The first is the business office; (*) indicates proper office to send manuscripts; (s) indicates a studio; at times all three may be at one address.

AMERICAN FILM MFG. CO., 6227 Broadway, Chicago (s); Santa Barbara, Calif. (*) (s).

BALBOA AMUSEMENT PROD. CO., Long Beach, Calif. (*) (s).

BIOGRAPH COMPANY, 807 East 175th St., New York City, (*) (s); Georgia and Girard, Los Angeles (s).

CALIFORNIA M. P. C., San Rafael, Calif. (*) (s).

THOS. A. EDISON, INC., 2826 Decatur Ave., New York City (*) (s).

EQUITABLE MOTION PICTURE CORP., 130 West 46th St., New York City. (*) Fort Lee, N. J. (s).

ESSANAY FILM MFG. CO., 1333 Argyle St., Chicago (*) (s).

FAMOUS PLAYERS FILM CO., 128 West 56th St., New York City (s) (*).

FOX FILM CORPORATION, 130 West 46th St., New York City (*); Los Angeles (s); Fort Lee, N. J. (s).

GAUMONT COMPANY, 110 West 40th St., New York City (*); Flushing, N. Y. (s); Jacksonville, Fla. (s).

DAVID HORSLEY STUDIO, Main and Washington, Los Angeles (*) (s).

KALEM COMPANY, 235 West 23d St., New York City (*); 251 W. 19th St., New York City (s); 1425 Fleming St., Hollywood, Calif. (s); Tallyrand Ave., Jacksonville, Fla. (s); Glendale, Calif. (s).

GEORGE KLEINE, 805 E. 175th St., N. Y. City (*).

LASKY FEATURE PLAY CO., 485 Fifth Ave., New York City; 6284 Selma Ave., Hollywood, Calif. (*) (s).

LONE STAR FILM CORPORATION, Los Angeles, Calif., (Chaplin).

LUBIN MFG. CO., 20th and Indiana, Philadelphia (*); Broad and Glenwood, Philadelphia (s); Coronado, Calif. (s); Jacksonville, Fla. (s).

METRO PICTURES CORP., 1476 Broadway, New York City (*). (All manuscripts for the following studios go to Metro's Broadway address): Rolfe Photoplay Co. and Columbia Pictures Corp., 3 West 61st St., New York City (s); Popular Plays and Players, Fort Lee, N. J. (s); Quality Pictures Corp., Metro office.

OLIVER MOROSCO PHOTOPLAY CO., 222 West 42d St., New York City; 201 N. Occidental Blvd., Los Angeles. (*) (s).

PALLAS PICTURES, 220 West 42d St., New York City; 205 N. Occidental Blvd., Los Angeles (*) (s).

PATHE FRERES, Jersey City, N. J. (*) (s).

PATHE EXCHANGE, 25 West 45th St., New York City (*) (s).

SELIG POLYSCOPE CO., Garland Bldg., Chicago (*) (s); 3800 Mission Road, Los Angeles (s).

SIGNAL FILM CORP., Los Angeles, Calif (*) (s).

THANHOUSER FILM CORP., New Rochelle, N. Y. (*) (s); Jacksonville, Fla. (s).

TRIANGLE FILM CORPORATION, 1457 Broadway, New York City; Fine Arts Studio (Griffith) 4500 Sunset Blvd., Hollywood, Calif. (*) (s); Keystone Studio (Sennett), 1712 Alessandro St., Los Angeles (*) (s); Kay-Bee Studio (Inc.), Culver City, Calif. (*) (s).

UNIVERSAL FILM MFG. CO., 1600 Broadway, New York City; 573 Eleventh Ave., New York City (*) (s); Universal City, Calif. (*) (s); Coytsville, N. J. (s).

VITAGRAPH COMPANY OF AMERICA, East 15th and Locust Ave., Brooklyn, N. Y. (*) (s); Hollywood, Calif. (*) (s); Bay Shore, Long Island, N. Y. (s).

WHARTON, INC., Ithaca, N. Y. (*) (s).

WORLD FILM CORP., 130 West 46th St., New York City (*); Fort Lee, N. J. (s).

CLARA KIMBALL YOUNG FILM CORP., 126 W. 46th St., New York (*).

GLOSSARY

ADAPTATION—A photoplay built from published
fiction or fact.

ART DIRECTOR—One whose duties are to see to
it that any art objects in a "set" are correct as to
period, and that the decorations and embellishments
of interiors are in artistic harmony.

ATMOSPHERE—The impalpable but very real
ether of emotions which surrounds a scene or a
play; the essence of locale enwrapping it. Like all
vague descriptive terms, "atmosphere" is susceptible
of any of a dozen definitions, as may best suit the
fancy of the definer.

AUXILIARY CHARACTER—One other than any
of the chief characters of a photoplay.

BUNCH LIGHTS—A cluster of incandescents used
in "sets."

BUSINESS—Author's instructions as to how the
player shall act in specific places in the plot.

BUST—A term used to designate that only face and
shoulders are to be shown in a close-up view.

"CAMERA"—When a Director has his players, or
his momentarily unpeopled "set," about ready to
begin photographing, he calls sharply: "Camera!"
and the Cameraman must instantly have his scene in
perfect focus and himself ready to begin turning
the crank at the command "Shoot!"

CAMERA EYE—A person who in his mental viewing of a plot, scene, episode or incident can so visualize it as to determine correctly whether it would film effectively, is said to have the "camera eye."

CAPTION—Same as subtitle; an explanatory line or lines relating to certain scenes or parts of a photoplay.

CAST—The players composing a company, and the respective characters of the photoplay they interpret.

CHARACTER—One of the supposititious persons in a screen story.

CLOSE-UP—The photographic enlargement of any fragment of a scene, present or previous, such as a face, or the passing of a finger across the page of an opened book underneath specific lines, or a watch held in the palm with the hands of it marking a crucial hour, etc., etc.

CONTINUITY—Logical progression of the action of a plot; absence of contradiction as scene succeeds scene.

COOPER-HEWITTS—The mercury-vapor lamps used (overhead) for photographing interior scenes. They diffuse an intense, steely-blue radiance which has the peculiar studio effect of making the features resemble those of a bloated corpse, swollen and mottled.

CUT-BACK—To return to and repeat a scene previously shown; or to return to a previous "set" and reuse it for a new scene.

CUT SCENE—A filmed scene which has been shortened by the Cutter after being viewed in the projection room; instruction to stop camera.

DENOUEMENT—The "now you've danced, pay the fiddler" part of the story which comes after the climax of the plot has been shown on the screen; the "settling up" aftermath of the plot; the final (moral or otherwise) justification of the story; the denouement may be pleasant or unpleasant as called for by the plot.

DIRECTOR—The person whose chief duty is to stand by and oversee the acting of the scenario by the players; to correct them where they are wrong or not up to their best, and generally to be on the job every minute to the end that the very best possible photoplay shall come out of the written plot. In action—that is to say, when scenes are being played or rehearsed before the camera—the Director is czar absolute; he duplicates the stage manager of the spoken drama. A Director General is one who has under him the Directors, of whom a large producing company may have a staff of a dozen or twenty.

DIRECTOR OF LOCATION—The person whose duty it is to scour the countryside and find suitable sites or locations for the purposes of the photoplay to be made; he generally has a list of these on hand, card-indexed, against emergency.

DISCOVER—To become conscious of the presence in a scene of a character already upon the scene.

DISSOLVE—To melt one picture into another without any withdrawal of the first from the screen.

EPISODE—An incident arising out of the plot but not a part of the plot, introduced to give variety and quickstep to the plot's unfoldment; one of a series of separate yet related stories.

ESTABLISH—To register in a broader sense: Thus, a player will be ordered by the Director to "register" wrath, and to "establish" triumph, or innocence, or guilt.

EXHIBITOR—The person who operates the theatre or other place where the moving picture is shown.

EXIT, EXEUNT—Former, the going of one character off the photo-stage; latter, of more than one character.

EXTERIOR—An out-of-doors setting.

FADE—The word "fade" is used in two compound forms: Fade-in and Fade-out. The former is a scenario direction to dissolve into a scene while being shown on the screen some other picture, such as the face of the heroine in reminder of a previous happening; to fade-out is to dissolve the scene on the screen into blackness.

FEATURE—A "feature play" is one, seldom less than four reels in length, which either deals with some unusual subject in a more or less original way, or deals with some more or less original subject in an unusual way; the term, however, is extremely elastic and has been much abused, often being applied erroneously in place of "spectacle" play. Example: "Brewster's Millions."

FILM—(1) A chemically sensitized strip of celluloid upon which the actions of the players, and their surroundings, are photographically registered; (2) a photoplay; (3) to turn a story into a photoplay.

FLASH—The throwing upon the screen for a fragment of a moment of a scene or character or other component part of the plot, to heighten the effect of the immediate scene.

FLASH-BACK—A fragment of a previous scene reflashed on the screen to intensify or clarify the scene being shown.

FREE-LANCE—A photoplay writer who is under contract or engagement to no producing company, but submits his scenarios where and when he wills.

GESTURE—To register by body pantomime instead of by facial expression.

INSERT—(noun) A writing, such as a letter, telegram or newspaper clipping, thrown upon the screen between scenes to reimpress some action which has gone before; (verb) corresponding.

INTERIOR—An indoors setting.

INTERPOSE—To break in abruptly upon the orderly progression of incidents and show something unrelated to the immediate sequence but which emphasizes a turn of the plot.

LEAD—The principal part in a photoplay cast.

LEADER—The caption, or explanatory line, which precedes the first scene on the screen. Subsequent lines of this character are called "subtitles."

LENS LOUSE—A vulgar but much used name for a player who snatches at every opportunity to obtrude himself in the camera foreground.

LOCATION—The out-of-doors place where and whereabout a photoplay or part of it is being made. When a company is thus engaged it is said to be "on location."

LOT—The enclosed grounds around the studio building or buildings.

MULTIPLE REEL—A photoplay of more than one reel.

OFF—The reverse of "On."

ON—When a player is "in a set," or before the camera, he or she is said to be "on;" that is to say, on the stage.

OPPOSITE—When a female part is cast as a foil to a male leading part, or vice versa, the person who plays the foil part is said to be acting "opposite" the lead.

PAD—To "pad" a story (scenario) is to inject into it unnecessary matter in order to lengthen it.

PANTOMIME—Screen action by movements of the limbs or other portions of the body, or by the features, to convey meaning.

PHOTOPLAY—A story told in motion pictures.

PICTURE STORY—A photoplay.

PLOT—The characters, and happenings in their sequence, around and upon which the scenario is built.

PORTABLE LIGHTS—A stand or rack of mercury lights of an intensity like white-hot steel, fed by a pliable cable so that they can be lifted and carried from point to point of the studio "set" as desired; they may be used alone or in conjunction with the Cooper-Hewitts; one of their chief advantages is that they can be carried to any exterior point—any place beyond the studio buildings—for use in taking night interiors, thus doing away with the necessity of photographing night interiors in the daytime and tinting the film pale blue or amber to make it appear as night on the screen. The intensity of these portable lights is so severe that the players' eyes become painfully swollen and almost blinded if they have to endure them long at a time.

PROPS—Abbreviation of properties, the movable objects used in preparing "sets" for scenes. Also the studio name of the man who has charge of the care of these objects, the Property Man.

PUNCH (noun)—To "put the punch into" a scene or play is to inject into it action which will stir strong emotion, of one kind or another.

READING—An examination, perusal, of a submitted scenario or synopsis, or both, by the Scenario Editor's department.

REEL—Approximately 1,000 feet of film.

REGISTER—To portray by the expression of the features a given emotion, as hate, love, joy, anger, benevolence, grief, etc.

RELEASE—Surrender of a photoplay to exhibitors for exhibition on an understood date.

SCENARIO—The written form from which the photoplay is filmed, or produced.

SCENARIO EDITOR—The chief of the Scenario Staff.

SCENARIO STAFF—The writers and readers of photoplays comprising a corps under employment by a film-producing company.

SCENE—Portrayal of a situation by the camera between the time when it is focused and the time when it is moved to another point.

SCREEN—The space, whether cloth-covered or whitened wall, upon which the film images are thrown and move.

'SCRIPT—Abbreviation of manuscript; the written form of the plot and its related instructions for producing.

SERIAL—A photoplay made up of too many reels to be presented at one performance and which hence is presented in installments, commonly not less than one week apart.

SET—The arrangement of articles of furniture, background, decorations, etc., for the enactment of a scene or scenes.

SEQUENCE—The orderly, or logical, procedure of. the events and situations of a plot, each progressive of the one preceding.

"SHOOT"—When the Director is ready for the Cameraman to begin photographing a scene, he calls sharply: "Shoot!"

SITUATION—The temporary state or relation of affairs at a point in the development of the plot.

SLAPSTICK COMEDY—Comedy of the horseplay sort.

SPECTACLE—A photoplay embracing scenes of gorgeousness or great splendor or unusual numbers of participants, designed to impress the eye and. mind with its lavishness, its hugeness, or its pretentious splendor. Examples: "Judith of Bethulia," "The Birth of a Nation."

SPLIT REEL—One-half of a reel, or approximately 500 feet of film. A short "filler" play.

STAFF READER—One of the Scenario Editor's assistants; one who reads submitted scenarios and passes initial judgment on their native worth or adaptability to the present needs of the company employing him—or her.

STAR—A leading actor or actress who has risen to such heights of popular favor (or is intended so to rise by the employer) that he heads his own company, under the producing firm's direction.

STORY—Same as plot.

STUDIO—The place, inside or outside of walls, where a photoplay is made.

SUBTITLE—Explanatory lines thrown from time to time upon the screen to help keep clear the thread of the story.

SUSPENSE (One of the most vital principles of plot-building)—The keeping of the audience in doubt as to what will be the outcome of a situation, incident or series of events already shown and of major importance to the development of the story.

SYNOPSIS—A compact *resumé* of the story as elaborated in the scenario.

TECHNICAL DIRECTOR—One whose duties it is to see that no inconsistencies of inanimate detail creep into a "set." For example, if the scene calls for the wearing of the uniform of a soldier of a certain army of a certain period, the uniform must be exactly correct—not eleven buttons or nine, but ten, if ten were originally worn. A Technical Director never would have permitted a *certified milk bottle* to appear on the *ante bellum* sideboard when Dustin Farnum played "Cameo Kirby" at Louisville!

TECHNIQUE—The method employed in filming the story.

TINT—Passing daylight films through pale blue or amber coloring solutions to transform them (on the screen) into night scenes.

THRILLER—Another name for a melodramatic scene, reel or play. Commonly applied to a class of plays.

VISION—A striking and premeditated pose by one or more characters picturing the climax of a series of progressive scenes just ended.

Lightning Source UK Ltd.
Milton Keynes UK
UKHW010640290421
382834UK00001B/148